DATE DUE

Sentenced to Death

Sentenced to Death

The American Novel and Capital Punishment

David Guest

University Press of Mississippi
Jackson

America

lelines for permanence and durability of the
for Book Longevity of the Council on Library

)lication Data

Guest, David.
    Sentenced to death : the American novel and capital punishment /
by David Guest.
        p.   cm.
    Includes bibliographical references and index.
    ISBN 0-87805-917-2 (cloth : alk. paper)
    1. American fiction—20th century—History and criticism.   2. Law
and literature—United States—History—20th century.   3. Legal
stories, American—History and criticism.   4. Capital punishment in
literature.   5. Dreiser, Theodore, 1871–1945. American tragedy.
6. Wright, Richard, 1908–1960. Native son.   7. Capote, Truman,
1924– In cold blood.   8. Norris, Frank, 1870–1902. McTeague.
9. Mailer, Norman. Executioner's song.   I. Title.
PS374.L34G84   1997
813'.509355—dc20   96-30603
                                                          CIP

British Library Cataloging-in-Publication Data available

FOR BETH GUEST,
EMILY ELIZABETH GUEST,
AND CONNOR ALLEN GUEST

CONTENTS

ACKNOWLEDGMENTS

I could not have written this book had I not received help and encouragement from many people. I am especially indebted to the faculty, students, staff, and administrators of Austin Peay State University. Professors Vereen Bell, Jay Clayton, Sam Girgus, Phyllis Frus, and Ann Coughlin, all of Vanderbilt University, provided valuable criticism and direction in the earliest stages of the composition process. Professors Fred Ashe, Buck Beliles, Ken Cooper, Adam Meyer, and Caroline Woidat also helped me formulate and revise my argument through casual conversation and careful scrutiny of the work-in-progress. In the final stages of writing, I received insightful and helpful commentary from Professor David S. Reynolds. The monumental task of guiding the book from manuscript to publication would never have been accomplished without the hard work of Seetha A-Srinivasan and Anne Stascavage, of the University Press of Mississippi. To each of these people I offer my sincere thanks.

Finally, and most of all, I want to thank my wife, who endured far more than she should have to make this book possible.

INTRODUCTION

Capital punishment in the United States has undergone a series of drastic transformations in the twentieth century. In 1900, executions were relatively frequent. People were executed for a relatively wide variety of crimes. In the first three decades of the century the nation executed, on average, more than 100 people per year. The figure rose, reaching a peak of 199 in 1935. Most of those executed were convicted killers, but some had committed rape, armed robbery, kidnapping, and even burglary.

Over the next three decades, the death penalty was used with decreasing frequency and was restricted, in practice and sometimes in the statutes, to fewer and fewer crimes. In the midsixties executions dwindled and ceased: there were forty-two in 1961, seven in 1965, and two in 1967. In 1965, too, for the first time all of those executed were convicted murderers. Thereafter for almost a decade the death penalty went unused, but since 1977 there has been a rapid expansion in the population on Death Row and a gradual but accelerating rise in the annual number of executions. In 1977, there were just over 400 people on Death Row nationwide; today the figure is above 2,700. Execution now appears to be reserved for murderers, but annual totals for executions are once again approaching the 100 mark.

The advance, retreat, transformation, and return of capital punishment have to some extent been dictated by the courts but have also reflected fluctuations in public attitudes toward the death penalty and public understanding of it. Occasionally, for example, there has been a surge in popular support for its abolition; between 1907 and 1917, nine states passed legislation abolishing the death penalty completely or almost completely. Between 1953 and 1966, Gallup polls showed support for capital punishment falling from 68 percent to 45 percent ("Death for the Death Penalty?"). More recently, the trend has reversed. By 1995, the figure had climbed as high as 75 percent. Perhaps even more striking is the shift in popular opinion about the appropriate use of the death penalty. Public support for the execution of burglars has all but disappeared.

If we widen our scope to include the nineteenth century, similar and even more dramatic fluctuations are evident. There has been a clear trend toward reducing the variety of capital crimes. Executions for sodomy, arson, theft, and counterfeiting ceased gradually, although not all states bothered to repeal the relevant statutes. The ritual itself changed fundamentally. Although in the early decades of the century, criminals were put to death publically, often while thousands watched, as the century advanced, the penalty began to be administered behind closed doors. At an 1827 execution in Cooperstown, New York, so many viewers filled the bleachers that a section collapsed, killing two. On another occasion that same year the crowd numbered between 30,000 and 40,000 (Friedman, 76). In the 1830s, states began conducting executions in more or less private settings behind prison walls. Public spectacles became increasingly rare, although the change came gradually, and they were not prohibited by law throughout the nation until 1937 (Bedau, 13).

The transformation of capital punishment in the nineteenth century represented but one element of a broader revolution in the cultural response to crime. The precise nature and extent of the reforms is disputed but not their general shape. At the beginning of the century, prisons functioned primarily to hold people awaiting trial. By century's end, the penitentiary system housed a growing population of convicted felons serving prescribed sentences. During the century confinement superseded punishments of the body. Torture, mutilation, flogging, and public humiliation in the stocks fell into disuse.

Beginning with Tennessee in 1838, states adopted discretionary sentencing procedures rather than mandatory ones, so that judges and juries could tailor the punishment, within limits, to the particular offender. As late as midcentury, the nation had no permanent police forces. By the end of the century, however, all large cities boasted "modern" police forces, and smaller cities and towns had begun to follow suit. Probation and parole, important components of the twentieth-century criminal justice system, first saw widespread use in the nineteenth. The United States was so innovative in its reforms that European nations often sent emissaries—like Alexis de Tocqueville and Gustave de Beaumont—to study the criminal justice system as a model for reforms abroad.

The changes, planned on a grand scale, reflected more than a series of legal decisions. Many of the significant ones in fact took effect without alterations in the penal code, as when states ceased to demand the death penalty for some capital crimes, like sodomy or adultery, that remained on the books. Dramatic changes in the letter and the practice of criminal law inevitably indicate that cultural work is being done, that a paradigm shift is occurring in the understanding of crime, criminals, and police power. It is difficult to specify how, why, and where such work takes place, but the results are readily summarized. For the most part, the correctional system today has little to do with violent, hardened convicts and even less to do with capital punishment.

In our time the United States has begun imprisoning a higher percentage of its population than any other nation. Between 1880 and 1983, the number of state and federal prison inmates grew from 30,000 to 419,000, while the incarceration rate per 100,000 almost tripled, from 61 to 179 (Friedman, 460). By 1995, the prison population topped 1 million. Between 1980 and 1995, the nation's total inmate population—the number of inmates in state and federal prisons combined with those in local jails—tripled, rising to 1.5 million, a number that seemed constrained only by the pace of prison construction. During the same fifteen-year period, the incarceration rate per 100,000 rose from 139 to 387. Perhaps most striking is the fact that in the summer of 1995 the nation's total correctional population, which includes the incarcerated as well as those on probation and on parole, topped 5 million, or 2.7 percent of the general population (United States Department of Justice).

Such statistics are relatively straightforward; attempts to map the connections between the sprawling criminal justice system (including police, jail, court, probation, parole, and prison systems) and the culture that informs it are less so. The system's existence attests to some sort of enabling discourse, but it is hard to trace. Does it, for example, lie only in the penal code and in the transcripts of trials and sentencing proceedings? Certainly, procedural rules authorize every official action taken by agents of our criminal justice system, and the penal code determines which acts are criminal offenses. Each crime, each criminal, and each judgment produce their own documentation, strands in the web of discourse through which correctional power is exerted. But does the cultural work that undergirds the correctional system take place only in these official texts?

A vast body of public discourse surrounds the subject of capital punishment. It elicits support and opposition from many quarters. Execution has long been justified as a sometimes appropriate punishment, as a deterrent, and even as evidence that society places supreme value on human life. Rhetoric pro and contra sometimes addresses the general question of mandated death and sometimes focuses on the details of a particular case.

The public discussion of crime and punishment, however, encompasses more than the penal code and debates about courts, judges, and juries. The modern criminal justice system emerged at the same time as the fields of psychiatry, criminology, sociology, anthropology, and psychology. These disciplines purported to apply scientific methods of inquiry to behavior, mental illness, and the social and psychological dimensions of crime. Credentialed scientists of the mind increasingly served as expert witnesses in trials, and press coverage of their testimony introduced new theories and a new language into the public discussion of crime.

The emergence of the modern criminal justice system coincided as well with a shift in the news media and in popular writing. At the beginning of the nineteenth century, newspapers covered crime little or not at all. Within a few decades, however, it had become a staple of journalism, particularly of the penny press. Notorious murder trials, like the 1836 trial of Richard Robinson for the murder of Helen Jewett, and the 1841 trial of John Colt for the murder of Samuel Adams, boosted circulation and helped make the penny newspaper a fixture of the American scene. Nineteenth-century publishers also produced and marketed books, broadsides, and pamphlets in unprecedented numbers. Many of these narratives recount the exploits of infamous criminals and carry suggestive illustrations as well as the obligatory denunciations of vice. In the era of public executions, spectators often had the opportunity to purchase biographies, autobiographies, and death-cell confessions of the condemned. These genres continued to appear even after public executions ceased. Today crime is as regular a feature of the news media as weather or sports. Sensational capital cases are increasingly the subject of "gavel-to-gavel" broadcasts, talk shows, mass-market "True Crime" books, and made-for-television movies.

The growth of nonfiction writing about crime and punishment has found a parallel in fiction. Capital murder today stands at the center of genres ranging from the genteel cerebral mystery to the courtroom melodrama to the hard-boiled crime thriller to mainstream or serious fiction. In one sense, crime fiction is nothing new. Violent murder has a long literary history. But in the nineteenth century the vocabulary used to describe it expanded rapidly. Newspapers brought the language of psychiatry, sociology, and criminology to a wide audience. The rhetorical conventions of the new disciplines found their way into realist and naturalist novels.

During the last century the new sciences of the mind have increasingly shaped the relationship between public discourse and correctional power because of their increasingly influential role within the criminal justice system. The prerequisite for discretionary sentencing is a diagnosis—an individualized assessment of culpability, potential for rehabilitation, and dangerousness—and also an appraisal of the circumstances surrounding each crime. As a result a new genre has emerged: the diagnostic biography, a life story that tells how the individual's impulse to wrongdoing originated and evolved. Most often, such biographies are employed to set the length of a sentence or to evaluate candidates for early release, but in capital cases they inform decisions of life or death.

The diagnostic biography of the capital criminal has a fictional counterpart that may be termed the execution novel, which is the subject of the present book. Execution novels tell the story of a life that leads to the gallows (or to the electric chair, the gas chamber, the firing squad, or the injection table). A list of such novels might include Herman Melville's *Billy Budd* (1891; pub. 1924), Theodore Dreiser's *An American Tragedy* (1925), Upton Sinclair's *Boston* (1928), Ward Greene's *Death in the Deep South* (1936), Richard Wright's *Native Son* (1940), James M. Cain's *The Postman Always Rings Twice* (1934), Willard Motley's *Knock on Any Door* (1947), Truman Capote's *In Cold Blood* (1965), William Bradford Huie's *The Execution of Private Slovik*, (1954), William Styron's *The Confessions of Nat Turner* (1966), E.L. Doctorow's *The Book of Daniel* (1971), Robert Coover's *The Public Burning* (1976), and Norman Mailer's *The Executioner's Song* (1979). If the parameters of the genre are extended slightly to include novels that focus on capital murder cases or trials but do not end in lawful executions, the list stretches to include works as various as Frank Norris's *McTeague* (1899), Meyer Levin's *Compulsion* (1956), Joseph Wambaugh's *The Onion Field* (1973), and Harper Lee's *To Kill a Mockingbird* (1960).

I argue that the nonliterary public discourse of crime and punishment provides a context for reading the execution novel that is at least as important as the context supplied by literary tradition. My purpose is not to explore capital punishment as a theme of the execution novel, or to set execution novels against other works of literature, but instead to examine these novels as part of the discourse that enables both capital punishment and the criminal justice system. Because my subject is the relationship between discourse about prisons and the power to imprison, I focus on execution novels that treat "the crime problem." This emphasis on the relationship between popular images of crime and public policy means that I exclude from consideration novels like *The Book of Daniel* and *The Public Burning*, both of which deal with the 1953 executions of "atomic spies" Julius and Ethel Rosenberg, and novels that focus on military or maritime justice, like *Billy Budd* and *The Execution of Private Slovik*. My concern, in other words, is with public perceptions of crime and criminality. In addition I have chosen to concentrate on execution novels that are not complicated by questions of wrongful conviction or mistaken identity, as are *Boston, Death in the Deep South,* and *To Kill a Mockingbird*. Such novels focus on cases in which the criminal justice system fails to function as intended, whereas I focus here on the system's normal functioning. I have therefore chosen execution novels that closely resemble official diagnostic biographies in form and intent.

Such novels most commonly reflect the traditions of naturalism and social realism. They share with diagnostic biography the assumption that a crime is best understood in light of the life and mind of the person who committed it. These novels attempt much the same task that Michel Foucault attributes to the medical experts and alienists whose testimony plays such a vital role in capital trials: "The doctors . . . began now to be called upon as 'specialists in motivation'; they had to evaluate not only the subject's reason but also the rationality of the act, the whole system of relationships which link the act to the interests, the plans, the character, the inclinations, and the habits of the subject" ("The Dangerous Individual," 138–39).

The five execution novels that I have selected are closely linked to real-life capital cases. The author of each of the novels—*McTeague, An American Tragedy, Native Son, In Cold Blood,* and *The Executioner's Song*— has identified it with a particular capital murder case, and each novel purports to present a realistic, unbiased, and clinically accurate account of murder as a phenomenon. *In Cold Blood* and *The Executioner's Song* present themselves as hybrid forms blending fiction with nonfiction. All of the novels but *McTeague* end with executions. I argue that *McTeague*'s ending represents a naturalized form of execution. Each of the five novels addresses a capital crime in which the identity of the killer is known and in which the central question is thus not guilt or innocence but criminal responsibility. The novels approach this question as the sentencing phase of a capital trial would, by attempting to determine the killer's state of mind and degree of self-control at the time of the killings.

All too often studies of these novels have limited themselves to literary connections. *McTeague,* for example, is typically measured against Zola and the European naturalists. Ronald Schleifer has argued that *The Executioner's Song* is Mailer's rewriting of *An American Tragedy* and to a lesser extent of *In Cold Blood* and that this rewriting was guided by Mailer's vision of opposing genteel and populist literary traditions. Robert M. Arlett, in "The Veiled Fist of a Master Executioner," links the role of the executioner and the role of the artist in several of Mailer's works; he focuses on *The Executioner's Song* and an earlier poem of the same title. Studies that limit themselves to literary works have tended to emphasize the execution novel's "realism" and "objectivity" or to characterize such novels as explorations of literary questions concerning, say, representation and point of view. Exclusively literary studies have their place, but there is no reason to believe that novelists read (or rewrite) only other novelists. A novel written about capital punishment enters into the contemporaneous public discussion of crime underway in newspapers, magazines, pulp fiction, and other media. By establishing connections between these novels and some of the writings that inform them, I hope to restore at least a portion of their original extraliterary context.

In the past when a novel's extraliterary context has been considered, it has usually been argued that many, if not all, novels about crime resist or subvert the dominant discourse about incarceration. *Native Son* was often regarded as participating in the public debate over crime. Sally Day Trigg's "Theodore Dreiser and the Criminal Justice System in *An American Tragedy*," to take another example, treats Dreiser's novel as a kind of editorial attacking the injustices and inconsistencies of capital punishment in America.

Other versions of the subversive approach range from the extreme (literature is inherently subversive) to more moderate claims (the literature of crime represents a subversive strain in the literary imagination). Both David S. Reynolds's *Beneath the American Renaissance* and Thomas Boyle's *Black Swine in the Sewers of Hampstead*, for example, link sensational writing about crime and more mainstream or canonical fictional works and then argue on the basis of these connections for the existence of a continuing tradition of subversive literary imagination. Naturalist novels often seem rooted in the subversive paradigm because of their treatment of determinism and not merely because of their sensationalism. When they trace the deterministic forces that lead a person inexorably toward a crime, they oppose the dominant discourse by downplaying the criminal's responsibility for his or her actions.

In my opinion such subversive paradigms form part of a romantic tradition that views the artist as somehow removed from society and political power, as a seer able to observe and critique society with privileged vision. In the subversive model, the novelist becomes an especially insightful social critic, one who sets the work of sociologists, psychologists, and anthropologists within a popular narrative form. This privileging of literature is even retained, as Frank Lentricchia has argued, in much of the "new historicism": "The literary historicist (old and new) grants literature precisely what historicist theory (especially new-historicist theory, with its emphasis on the constitutive presence of the historical reader) is not supposed to grant to any distinct cultural form: the very power which formalist theory claims for literature, the unique privilege of putting us into authentic contact with the real thing through the medium of the 'great writer' and his canonical texts" (89). Once we view the novel as part of a broader discursive context, however, its subversive aspect is less apparent than its enabling function. I presuppose, of course, that the exercise of power requires an enabling discourse with a tendency to obscure its own true function: that is, discourse on the subject of prisons achieves its goals by appearing disinterested and objective.

Execution novels take on new and sometimes unexpected meaning when they are considered alongside the diagnostic biography of the executable offender. If we know that a certain narrative or biographical version of the capital criminal's life must be produced in order for execution to take place, is it not possible that novels about those same executions participate in, or become entangled with, this enabling discourse at the systemic level? If so, far from being aloof and detached from society, the execution novel and the literary artist both participate in and mirror a discourse that facilitates the exercise of power.

In other words, the discursive context can change the way we think about the realist and naturalist novel. The reverse may be true as well. Execution novels focus on the site and the application of socially approved police force and thereby scrutinize one of the least studied and most potent determinants of the nation's social history. Although we in the United States commit and punish crimes at a rate far exceeding those of other Western nations, the history of our criminal justice system remains largely unwritten and utterly absent from the school textbook and the encyclopedia. In the 1,200 oversized, densely printed pages of the encyclopedic *Reader's Companion to American History*, hundreds of pages expound military and political topics, but the entry on crime, at three pages, is shorter than the two entries devoted to "domestic work." Prisons merit three passing references (one in the entry on architecture), as does basketball. There are no entries for capital punishment, the death penalty, jail, probation, or parole.

The historical invisibility of the criminal justice system is especially noteworthy, given its conspicuous presence in contemporary culture. The military may dominate the history books, but the police hold sway in the media. In political races, too, opponents routinely compete with one another to see who can denounce crime and criminals more vigorously. The hyperbolic rhetoric widens the gap between the work of the criminal justice system and the citizens' perception of it. The public forum is increasingly dominated by images of the electric chair, the gas chamber, and the injection table, by the maximum security prison and the hardened convict who, once on parole, only continues his predatory lifestyle.

The diagnostic biography of the capital offender incorporates the two aspects of criminal justice—one visible but largely symbolic, the other invisible but active. Such narratives mirror and shape the exercise of power by tracing the offense to its origins in a broad range of criminal and antisocial behaviors. These diagnostic narratives, being rooted in the social and psychiatric sciences, also exhibit, in a way consistent with the principles of literary realism and naturalism, a legitimizing rhetoric that professes clinical detachment and scrupulous devotion to truth. Put simply, the more we know about the rhetoric of the execution novel, the more we know about the mythic underpinnings of our nation's unprecedented experiment in incarceration.

Sentenced to Death

How could power exercise its highest prerogatives by putting people to death, when its main role was to ensure, sustain, and multiply life, to put this life in order? For such a power, execution was at the same time a limit, a scandal, and a contradiction. Hence capital punishment could not be maintained except by invoking less the enormity of the crime itself than the monstrosity of the criminal, his incorrigibility, and the safeguard of society. One had the right to kill those who represented a kind of biological danger to others.

—Michel Foucault

If clothes make the man, then words make the monster.

—Caryl Chessman writing from Death Row

ONE

Power, Narrative, and Capital Punishment

The diagnostic biography of the executable offender has a characteristic rhetoric that suits its purpose. Discretionary sentencing requires judges and juries to decide between life and death—to choose the one person who will be executed from a group of ten or fifty or two hundred people convicted of the same offense. A profile of the executable offender will be established, capital felons will be measured against that profile, and a small percentage of these felons will be chosen to die. The official discourse must establish the state's authority and ability to detain, judge, and punish the offender. A candidate for the death penalty must demonstrably have violated the social contract so completely that his or her life is forfeit. In addition, the offender must be proven to have been legally sane at the time of the crime so that he or she may be held responsible for it. In a more general sense, the discourse must show that justice is blind, that judgment is both impartial and fair, and that it is possible in a meaningful way to differentiate the few who deserve to die from the thousands convicted of capital crimes each year who will continue to live.

The criminal justice system as a whole also has an enabling discourse of this kind to justify its actions. In this respect the war on crime resembles military war: the state's efforts are buttressed by texts that dehumanize its enemies while glorifying its standard-bearers. It becomes important to differentiate the "true" criminal from the law-abiding citizen. The capital offender stands at the heart of this discourse as the criminal so dangerous and so irredeemable—so threatening to the social order—that he or she must be destroyed.'

By a curious irony, as the convicted and the condemned become less and less visible to the public, as they are increasingly confined and executed behind prison walls, they come more and more to be known through written narratives, which then dominate public discussions of crime and criminal policy. When capital punishment is meted out less and less frequently, the executed few seem all the more monstrous. As executions become less visible, and known to the public only at second hand, the capital offender attains symbolic, indeed mythic, significance.

I rely here on Roland Barthes's definition of myth as "depoliticized speech." In "Myth Today," Barthes argues that myth "has the task of giving a historical intention a natural justification, and making contingency appear eternal. . . . What the world supplies to myth is a historical reality, defined, even if this goes back quite a while, by the way in which men have produced or used it; and what myth gives in return is a *natural* image of this reality. . . . myth is constituted by the loss of the historical quality of things; in it, things lose the memory that they once were made" (130–31). Racist myths, for example, have suppressed the historical contexts of slavery and political oppression, setting in their place biological (rather than social or political) explanations for disparities in the lives of white and black Americans.

The diagnostic biography of the capital offender embodies the myth of the psychopath. The psychopath has evolved under various names—moral imbecile, homicidal monomaniac, Lombrosian degenerate, sociopathic personality disorder—but throughout its transfor-

4

mations the central elements of the model have remained the same. Psychopaths, according to the myth, appear sane, at least to the civilian or nonprofessional, but lack the moral and empathic faculties that separate humans from animals. A particular set of historical, judicial, and political circumstances is presumed to have created the psychopath as profiled. The myth naturalizes the profile as a kind of medical condition—but the biographical narratives used to define and diagnose psychopathy typically omit (erase) the circumstances. Medical and correctional technologies enter such narratives only after the fact, as treatment reluctantly prescribed for a dangerous and innate criminality that can no longer be ignored.

If the idea that a widely accepted clinical category may be grounded in myth seems far-fetched, consider the history of psychiatry and the diagnosis of mental disorders. The nineteenth century produced distinguished doctors—including the Italian Cesare Lombroso, the German Ernest Kretschmer, and especially Emil Kraepelin—who regarded serious mental disorders as having biological causes and often genetic origins. Scientific ignorance regarding the physiological basis of insanity, however, meant that the first coherent explanation—the theory of Sigmund Freud—rested on life experiences. Two distinct approaches to mental illness (the Kraepelinian, or organic, which stressed biological causes and somatic treatments, and the Freudian, or functional, which stressed intrapsychic conflict) thus vied for the imprimatur of the medical community starting in the nineteenth century. The first, traditional approach was mainly used for psychotic patients, schizophrenics, and manic-depressives; the second (psychoanalysis and "talk therapy") was used primarily in the treatment of psychoneurotics. The divergence reflected a power struggle within the medical community that pitted neurologists against psychiatrists—and eventually psychiatrists against psychoanalysts (see Valenstein and Oppenheim).

The ascendency of psychoanalysts within psychiatry meant that psychoanalytic techniques received increasing attention. These were touted as significantly alleviating organic mental illness and could be practiced by individuals lacking training in medicine. The psychoanalytical approach employed basic concepts—the belief that the mind was organized into superego, ego, and id; the concepts of the oedipal complex and the defense mechanism—that lacked any basis in physical reality. As Elliot Valenstein has succinctly written, "Psychoanalysis never offered any possibility of helping significant numbers of institutionalized psychotic patients, but it had created an illusion of a growing body of knowlege that would eventually be able to attack that problem" (8). As we know, the psychoanalytic view became immensely influential in shaping popular opinion regarding the origins of mental illness.

In the last decades of the twentieth century, far more is known, and is becoming known, about the biological basis of psychological disorders (for example, see Solomon). The legacy of Freud and his psychoanalytic successors, however, remains evident in the orientation of modern psychotherapists, who, as described by Dawes, usually rely on intuitive insight rather than on the findings of scientific research. It is also evident in the *Diagnostic and Statistical Manual of Mental Disorders* (the *DSM-IV*), the basis for all clinical diagnoses, which sets forth symptomatic (and often impressionistic) behavioral criteria for different illnesses without embodying the latest biochemical research on brain dysfunction. The resulting system for classifying people who behave oddly by prevailing norms, while accepted by the medical profession, thus carries the appearance of knowledge or certainty while lacking a scientific foundation.

Myths owe much of their power to the rhetoric of science. Rhetorical demonstrations of clinical detachment and objectivity—as we see in the *DSM-IV*—lend credibility to such myths. Even as broad a discipline as criminology in its traditional form illustrates how a discourse that appears to be objective can participate in the discourse of power. W. Byron Groves and Michael J. Lynch have described the project of traditional criminology as follows: "From a traditional perspective crime is a function of individual or group aberration, and to solve the crime problem we can 1) intervene in the lives of individual criminals, 2) disperse groups which carry or condone criminal behavior, or 3) beef up the criminal justice system so that it can more effectively handle criminal violations" (8).

Traditional criminology thus contains an implied critique of the correctional system: it suggests that the system could always do more to fight crime, perhaps by adding to the police presence or doing more in the prisons to rehabilitate inmates. Under the aegis of science, traditional criminology both criticizes the criminal justice system and promotes its growth. If we locate the ultimate source of crime within the aberrant individual—in line with this old-style thinking—then the best way to fight crime is by policing and confining that individual.

Close examination of diagnostic criminal biography reveals that its self-proclaimed objectivity may be a rhetorical ploy—an effort to disguise myth as fact. By masking the exercise of power with the rhetoric of science, such biographies can pose as disinterested assessments of the criminal's soul or character that have been compiled for the sake of accurate sentencing and efficient rehabilitation. Upon closer inspection, however, these biographies invite us to reconstruct the offender as delinquent. The distinction between offender and delinquent is the difference between a criminal act and a criminal personality type—a shift that introduces the possibility of punishing a person for being "the sort of person who 'tends' to commit crimes" (Lentricchia, 85).

A heightened awareness of the rhetorical strategies of correctional and criminological writing might help us reassess literary treatments of crime. We might reexamine, for example, the role of determinism in diagnostic biography. Within diagnostic criminal biography, determinism binds the criminal act to the character of the person who committed it and thus helps establish the need for the maximum punishment. The diagnostic biography attempts "the integration of the act into the global behavior of the subject" (Foucault, "The Dangerous Individual," 139). Evidence that deterministic forces have shaped a subject's actions increases our sense of the subject's personal responsibility: "The more clearly visible this integration [between criminal act and global behavior], the more clearly punishable the subject. The less obvious the integration, the more it seems as if the act has erupted in the subject, like a sudden and irrepressible mechanism, and the less punishable the responsible party appears" (Foucault, "The Dangerous Individual," 139).

Literary treatments of determinism, which typically reflect the view that individuals should be held responsible only for voluntary actions, treat deterministic forces as reducing personal responsibility. Diag-

7

nostic biography, then, employs determinism in a manner that exactly contradicts the customary understanding of determinism in literary studies. An awareness of this fact, and of other narrative strategies associated with diagnostic biography, suggests fruitful new ways of reading execution novels.

Diagnostic biography forms part of the vast body of paperwork that is associated with state-sponsored executions in the twentieth-century United States. Transcripts of court proceedings in a capital case can run to tens, even hundreds, of thousands of pages, including the testimony of eyewitnesses, expert witnesses, victims, law enforcement officers, criminalists, doctors, and any surviving victims. Criminal psychologists contribute elaborate clinical profiles of the condemned, profiles used sometimes by the prosecution, sometimes by the defense. Transcripts of capital cases, together with the penal codes that define capital crimes, not only form the official discourse of capital punishment but literally enable each execution.

Psychiatry entered the judicial process as attempts were made to separate executable capital offenders from those who would be allowed to live. Early invocations of psychology involved challenges, usually unsuccessful, to rules governing the insanity defense. Through much of the nineteenth century and into the twentieth, insanity in the legal sense was considered to be readily recognizable by the nonspecialist. Even today, most states adhere to some version of the M'Naghten (or McNaughten) Rule, which holds that if a person knew, at the time of committing the act, that what he or she was doing was wrong, then that person was sane enough to be held criminally responsible.

The M'Naghten Rule with its straightforward, cut-and-dried approach reminds us that insanity is a legal, rather than a medical, concept. The M'Naghten Rule focuses on the criminal's knowledge, or *mens rea*, and presupposes that people are capable of acting in accordance with what they know. The pivotal notion, then, is the concept of self-control. We believe that we can control our behavior, at least generally speaking; the effects of illness or disease, on the other hand, are beyond our control by definition. The insanity plea, a defensive strategy, interposed illness (loss of control) as a mitigating factor in applications of the M'Naghten Rule.

8

The problem, of course, lay in differentiating the rational criminals from the irrational (insane). How should we treat the crime that was committed by someone with no prior history or symptoms of insanity? Certainly the crime itself could not be regarded as evidence of previously undiagnosed mental illness; this position—untenable as a matter of public policy—would mean allowing murder to go unpunished. Could the crime be a momentary aberration in the life of an individual who was otherwise demonstrably sane? If so, what do we mean by "sanity"? If the criminal knew better, why didn't he do better? Was his motive rational or irrational? Ignorance of the causes of human behavior was profound. This was not an area, however, in which society could comfortably tolerate either ignorance or ambiguity.

Lacking the scientific knowledge necessary to trace mental illness to its physiological origins, nineteenth-century psychiatrists took a symptom-oriented approach. They identified new categories of insanity, such as homicidal monomania and moral insanity, which isolated discrete areas in which people's knowledge (or self-control) might be deficient because of illness. Monomania, an elusive form of insanity, manifested itself in a single narrow area. Monomaniacs could thus appear sane and normal most of the time but would become obsessive, wildly irrational, and even homicidal in regard to one particular subject. The rational faculties of the moral imbecile could be entirely intact, but the moral faculties common to normal humans were totally lacking. In court, and in some state penal codes, these new categories sometimes led to an "irresistible impulse" test: "The idea was that certain conditions had the power to affect human emotions without necessarily destroying cognitive functions. The person is in the helpless grip of a force outside himself, borne along by a tornado of instinct or drive" (Friedman, 144). For the monomaniacal murderer or the moral imbecile, a single act of explosive violence might expose a lifetime of apparent normalcy as a masquerade. The new models of insanity explained (or, more accurately, failed to explain), in terms accessible only to experts, ways in which apparently sane individuals could commit utterly irrational crimes. Homicidal monomania permitted the construction of a diagnostic biography that matched a senseless crime to a particular personality type, a personality for which the unnatural was natural.

In practice, the new versions of the insanity plea had limited success. Very soon after the monomania model was introduced, it was put to the legal test in the 1844 murder trial of a Kentucky doctor named Abner Baker. Baker shot and killed his brother-in-law, Daniel Bates, after accusing him of carrying on an affair with Baker's wife. The accusations were apparently so unbelievable that Baker's lawyer decided on a plea of not guilty by reason of insanity. The chief obstacle to this defense strategy was Baker's apparent mental competence; he was sane enough, after all, to maintain a successful medical practice. Nevertheless, Baker's attorney called in a medical expert who testified that Baker was a homicidal monomaniac suffering from delusions limited to the topic of his wife's infidelity. The witness cited as evidence the fact that when Baker addressed this subject, his "eyes became singularly red and excited and obviously maniacal" (quoted in White, 228).

Baker's defense strategy failed, and he was executed in 1845, but not before eight members of the jury signed a petition requesting that he be pardoned. According to the petition, the signers "believed that the prisoner labored under insane delusion as to Bates when he shot him . . . but that they believed that he had capacity enough to determine between right and wrong generally" (quoted in White, 231). The new categories of partial insanity, however, were not always failures. Twenty-three years after Baker was hanged, in the Iowa case of *State v. Felter*, Felter, who had inexplicably murdered his wife, attempted a defense based on "homicidal mania." He was convicted, but the conviction was overturned by an appellate court. The court's opinion stated that both the medical and legal professions "now recognize the existence of such a mental disease as homicidal insanity" (quoted in Friedman, 145). Monomania and moral insanity thus entered the courtroom as defensive strategies, means of *preventing* execution; they extended the "protection" of an insanity plea to the apparently sane. In the process, however, they helped establish a pathological model of the executable offender.

The concepts of homicidal monomania and moral insanity, "pathological" conditions lacking a scientific basis, were discarded by the

medical profession more than one hundred years ago, but they sur-
vived as Lombrosian degeneracy and linger still in the image of the
psychopath or sociopath. It is noteworthy that their diagnosis de-
pended on biographical narrative rather than physical symptoms. A
diagnosis of mental illness based purely on biography is clearly more
subjective than one based on objective evidence, especially when the
subject in question is believed to have committed murder.

The potential influence of concepts such as the moral imbecile, the
monomaniac, and the psychopath on the sentencing phase of a capital case is apparent from the case of Randall Dale Adams. In 1977,
Adams was convicted of first degree murder in the shooting of a Dallas police officer. The conviction was based on eyewitness testimony.
During the penalty phase of the trial the prosecution relied exclusively on the testimony of two witnesses, both psychiatrists, who met
and briefly examined Adams after he had been arrested and charged
with murder. Dr. John T. Holbrook testified that Adams was a sociopath and explained: "They [sociopaths] tend to have little regard for
the general institution of society and they act strictly in terms of their
own personal needs, that which makes them feel good at the time. . . .
Well, when they commit murder it is usually to make them feel good
or it is a matter of convenience to eliminate a witness or to give them
time. It is purely a practical matter for them from their point of view
of the circumstances, it has nothing to do with passion or commit-
ment as we understand that" (quoted in Adams, Hoffer, and Hoffer,
120). Holbrook concluded by testifying that Adams was unlikely ever
to change and that he would "constitute a continuing threat to society" (121).

Dr. James Grigson, the other prosecution witness, confirmed the
diagnosis of sociopathy, adding that "on the scale of sociopathy,"
Adams was "at the very extreme, worse or severe end of the scale.
You can't get beyond that." Grigson explained that he based his diagnosis on Adams's failure to demonstrate "any type of guilt or remorse" (122). When Adams's attorney asked whether the diagnosis
was predicated on a finding of actual guilt, the doctor denied that the
charges against Adams had anything to do with his findings: "I don't
really know what all Mr. Adams has done, but I know he is a socio-

11

path" (122). Despite the apparently circular reasoning, the jury re-turned a sentence of death in less than half an hour.

Adams spent the next twelve years on Death Row, protesting his innocence to anyone who would listen. Several times he came within hours of execution. His sentence might have been carried out if it had not been for the efforts of filmmaker Errol Morris. In 1988, Morris released a documentary film about Adams's case, *The Thin Blue Line*. In the film, David Harris, the only witness against Adams, confesses to an offscreen interviewer that he, Harris, had killed the policeman and had lied so that Adams would be blamed for the murder. Adams, who had met Harris on the day of the murder, was not even in the car at the time of the shooting. The confession, along with the public outcry that followed, led to a review of Adams's case and eventually to his release.

The story of Randall Adams serves to demonstrate the persistence of the myth of the sociopath. Like the moral imbecile, the homicidal maniac, the Lombrosian degenerate, and the psychopath, the socio-path is incurable, inherently dangerous, and—to the untrained eye—indistinguishable from the normal human. Adams's story also dem-onstrates the ease with which such a psychological profile can be abused and can be made to support the state's case for execution.

Psychiatric evaluations also influence death sentences in subtler ways, as illustrated by the story of two related cases from Florida, *Gardner v. Florida* and *Brown v. Wainwright*. In 1977, the U.S. Supreme Court reversed the death sentence of Daniel Gardner. Gardner had been convicted of killing his wife. The jury had recommended a life sentence. After reading a psychological evaluation of the convicted man provided by the state's Department of Offender Rehabilitation, the trial judge overruled the jury's recommendation and sentenced Gardner to death. Only later did the defense learn of the report, which had improperly been left out of the trial record. Because the defendant had not had the opportunity to respond to the evaluation, the Supreme Court reversed the judge's ruling and restored the life sentence originally endorsed by the jury.

The second case, *Brown v. Wainwright*, was a 1980 class action filed on behalf of 123 inmates of Florida's Death Row by a group of anti-death penalty activists who discovered, almost by accident, that the state supreme court had requested and received psychological screening reports on the 123 plaintiffs during mandatory reviews of their death sentences. The plaintiffs claimed that these reports, written without their knowledge and kept outside of the trial records, had no place in the review process and were potentially prejudicial. Because the suit accused the supreme court justices of misconduct, few observers were surprised when it was dismissed, but mystery and controversy linger. In the weeks before the state supreme court heard the case, for example, all of the reports disappeared. The chief justice's law clerk later claimed that she had disposed of the reports; she thought she might have shredded them. She also said that she could not remember who had told her to do so (Von Drehle, 170). The U.S. Supreme Court refused to hear the case on appeal, but when the class action suit was dropped and the same argument was used on behalf of individuals, the death sentence was lifted in a number of cases.

In short, moral insanity and psychopathy, bad science or not, have proven quite effective at creating criminal personality types and have provided judges and juries with pathological models of the executable subject. In fleshing out these models, diagnostic biographies serve not only to construct executable subjects but also to define social norms for the benefit of society at large.

The programmatic study of crime and the criminal, increasingly necessitated by the modern prison system, helps establish the dangerous "other" against which normalcy is defined. According to Mark Seltzer, "the spread of normalizing strategies entails the production of abnormalities that must then be known, ordered, supervised, and reformed; and in this way, knowledge, discourse, and power are linked and extended into larger and larger fields" (154). Bruce Lincoln describes the process of normalization in terms of affinity and estrangement; through discourse, he observes, these sentiments are manipulated "so that groups of persons experience themselves as separate and different from other groups with whom they might potentially be associated" (10).

One possible inference is that the criminal justice system does not so much diagnose criminal delinquency as manufacture it. Indeed, virtually since their inception prisons have been charged with failing in the attempt to reform inmates and with further criminalizing

13

them. Foucault and other radical criminologists have characterized the fabrication of delinquency as the true function of the criminal justice system: "the prison, and no doubt punishment in general, is not intended to eliminate offences, but rather to distinguish them, to distribute them, to use them . . . to assimilate the transgression of the laws in a general tactics of subjection" (Foucault, *Discipline*, 272). The fabrication of delinquency is evident both in the way that the prison encourages recidivism and in the way that penal discourse legitimates the delinquent. David Garland, for example, has argued that "the prison produced the delinquent in a categorical or epistemological sense, by creating in the course of its practices, the category of 'the individual criminal' " (Garland, 148).

The dominant discourse accommodates delinquency in a "general tactics of subjection" largely by manipulating images of danger, and the aura of danger around the individual criminal greatly increases when the crime is defined in pathological terms. In the wake of homicidal monomania and capital crime, pathological models and diagnostic biography have come to inform virtually every level of penal discourse. As the pathological model of criminality extends from capital crimes to lesser offenses, it influences not only the setting of sentences but the serving of them as well.

John Bartlow Martin's *Break Down the Walls* (1954), a treatise on prison reform, illustrates the downward movement. Martin argues that the criminology and the criminal justice system must ultimately differentiate the "true criminal from the situational offender" (266). He identifies this "true criminal" as the psychopath and declares, "The only proper role of a psychiatrist in prison at present is to advise the classification board and the parole board—to make sure that the truly dangerous man is put into maximum security and that he is not paroled (Some murderers could be safely paroled tomorrow. Some burglars ought to be locked up for the rest of their lives.)" (275).

Pathological approaches to criminality tend to increase the danger associated with crime. With its stress on logic and predictability, the typical diagnostic biography of the psychopath amplifies the aura of danger by identifying petty crimes or other examples of antisocial behavior as precursors of monstrous crime. In this manner, all criminality and abnormal behavior becomes linked, at least potentially, to criminality in its most extreme form.

Max Nordau's *Degeneration* (1895) illustrates the use of traditional criminology to show how crime and delinquency threaten the very fabric of society. Nordau argues that Lombrosian degeneracy manifests itself not only in criminality but also in a number of noncriminal activities, particularly the "decadent" art forms seen at the end of a century. Degenerates, Nordau explains, have always existed, "but they formerly showed themselves sporadically, and had no role in the life of the whole community. It was only the vast fatigue which was experienced by the generation on which the multitude of discoveries and innovations burst abruptly, imposing upon it organic exigencies greatly surpassing its strength, which created favourable conditions under which these maladies could gain ground enormously, and become a danger to civilization" (537).

Robert Lindner's *Rebel Without a Cause: The Story of a Criminal Psychopath* (1944) also links delinquency with imminent public danger by means of moral insanity. Lindner's model of the psychopath recalls both homicidal monomania and Lombrosian degeneracy. It posits a criminal insanity thought to be lurking unseen in people who appear normal. Lindner, like Nordau, sees an almost apocalyptic danger:

> The last few years have witnessed the triumphant heavy-booted march of psychopathy not only over an entire continent but over every painfully-won tenet of what we call our civilization. And as when a stone is cast on still waters, the mononuclear psychopathic center has communicated its compulsive impulses outwardly to awaken latent psychopathy many times removed from the volcanic core.
>
> *This is the menace of psychopathy: The psychopath is not only a criminal; he is the embryonic Storm-Trooper; he is the disinherited, betrayed antagonist whose aggressions can be mobilized on the instant at which the properly-aimed and frustration-provoking formula is communicated by that Leader under whose tinseled aegis license becomes law, secret and primitive desires become virtuous ambitions readily attained, and compulsive behavior formerly deemed punishable becomes the order of the day.* [Lindner, *Rebel*, 16]

Danger of this magnitude, of course, requires action. Once again, by establishing that crime is somehow an intrinsic character trait, traditional criminology endorses the idea that a society deals best with the

15

danger of crime through strict enforcement of the law and the liberal use of incarceration.

The concept of pathological criminal delinquency, then, in addition to supporting normalization by making all things abnormal seem dangerous, allows for fuller policing of the normal:

> The existence of a delinquent class can be used to curb other kinds of illegalities in a number of ways. First of all, the police measures of supervision which it necessitates can be used for wider political purposes. Secondly, the predatory nature of delinquency makes it unpopular with other members of the working classes, who tend to call on the law as a protection and increasingly to shun law-breaking in itself. The myths of dangerousness which grow up around the criminal element add to this process of distancing and division. Finally, an awareness that imprisonment tends to bring about a subsequent identification with the criminal element gives people added reason to avoid taking any risks with the law and to distrust those who do. On this account then, the prison does not so much control the criminal as control the working class by creating the criminal. [Garland, 150]

The fabrication of delinquency helps create an efficient, normalized working class. Psychological profiles of criminally dangerous individuals in narrative form cluster various character traits and behaviors around the concept of dangerous criminality. Increasingly refined portraits of pathological criminality entail an increasingly refined portrait of law-abiding normalcy.

An examination of the day-to-day operations of the criminal justice system illustrates that the policing of the normal should be regarded as not only an ideological phenomenon but also a job description for the system's agents. The popular discourse of criminality, however, overrepresents aspects of police work that involve dangerous criminals and law enforcement, while obscuring aspects of police work that are directed at normalization. Traditional criminology and penology, for example, focus on prisons and prison inmates while leaving the jail system virtually invisible. Jails, which are used to hold people convicted of misdemeanors and offenders awaiting trial, usually afford brief or provisional confinement.

In *The Jail: Managing the Underclass in American Society* (1985), John Irwin notes that "since John Howard's historic report on English jails,

The State of the Prisons in England and Wales (1777), there have been perhaps a dozen other reports [on the jail system] . . . , whereas there are hundreds of studies on the prison" (xi). The disparity is even more remarkable in light of the fact that the number of people passing through U.S. jails in a given year is "at least thirty times the number handled by all state and federal prisons" (xi).

Irwin's studies of the jail system in the United States lead him to conclude that jails function primarily not to enforce the law but to regulate a certain segment of the poor, a segment marked by "detachment" and "disrepute." "These findings suggest that the basic purpose of the jail differs radically from the purpose ascribed to it by government officials and academicians. It is this: the jail was invented, and continues to be operated, in order to manage society's rabble. Society's impulse to manage the rabble has many sources, but the subjectively perceived 'offensiveness' of the rabble is at least as important as any real threat it poses to society" (2). The fact that "offensiveness" plays such a large role in determining who is arrested suggests that the jails and the police function to enforce normalcy as much as to enforce the law: "The study of . . . arrest samples also indicates that offensiveness, as much or more than crime seriousness, was what led to being arrested, held in jail until disposition, and then perhaps being sentenced to jail. . . . Finally, receiving a jail sentence was related more closely to offensiveness than to crime seriousness: 23 percent of the persons with moderate or high offensiveness were sentenced to jail, compared with only 8 percent of those convicted of medium or serious crimes" (40–41).

In short, the criminal justice system and its discourse are concerned not only with conceptually separating criminality from normalcy but also with physically policing the normal. The specter of the dangerous criminal creates the need for law enforcement technologies that in their actual operation have less to do with dangerous criminals than with members of the underclass who are regarded as abnormal, offensive, or irksome by the upper classes. The policing of the normal takes place largely outside the penal code; perceived offensiveness may play a significant role in the functioning of the criminal justice system, but it is not illegal. The criminal justice system also polices the normal by criminalizing forms of individual behavior that do not directly harm people or their property. Such crimes are commonly called moral crimes, consensual crimes, or victimless crimes, and the criminal justice system works hard to enforce the laws against such crimes. The most commonly prosecuted consensual crimes are drug crimes, drunkenness, disorderly conduct, vagrancy, prostitution, and gambling. Peter McWilliams's admittedly incomplete accounting of the annual expenditures for prosecuting consensual crimes totaled $50 billion as of 1993. That number includes an annual total of $29 billion to arrest and incarcerate drug offenders (183–84). As of 1993, 350,000 people had been incarcerated for consensual crime. In 1991, arrests for consensual crimes nationwide totaled 2,802,800 (McWilliams, 187). The criminalization of consensual behavior is usually justified as a kind of preemptive strike against the more predatory and violent crimes that supposedly follow from such behaviors. Diagnostic criminal biography supports the criminalization of consensual behavior by providing a pathological, and thus scientifically legitimate, basis for the connection. Such biographies demonstrate, for example, that the movement from marijuana use to heroin addiction to burglary, armed robbery, and murder, is a natural, organic, and thus inevitable movement.

At first glance, capital punishment might seem to play a very small role in the workings of a criminal justice system largely devoted to prosecuting petty and even victimless crimes. Although the pace of execution in the United States is quickening and the Death Row population is at an all-time high, execution remains a rare phenomenon. In a nation with a quarter of a billion people, where more than twenty thousand murder convictions are handed down annually, it is likely that fewer than a hundred offenders will be executed this year. I will argue, however, that although execution has become less and less significant as a punishment for heinous crimes, it has become more and more significant as a means of providing us with criminal monsters.

The parallels between the diagnostic biography of the capital offender and the five novels in question raise interesting and sometimes disturbing questions about the relationship between those novels—and perhaps the traditions of literary realism and naturalism from which they spring—and the myths that undergird our criminal

18

justice system. Like the myth of the psychopath, moral imbecile, or born criminal, *McTeague*, *An American Tragedy*, *Native Son*, *In Cold Blood*, and *The Executioner's Song* attempt to map the connections between capital crimes and capital offenders. In doing so, these novels may participate in the normalization of both the inherently criminal personality and the criminal justice system itself. If so, they not only participate in the dominant discourse but are accomplices to execution.

If a model of human behavior emerges to challenge the assumption that crime is located within certain dangerous individuals, then the dominant discourse must respond, either by rejecting the new model or by incorporating it. Barthes proposes "inoculation" as one strategy by which myth responds to potential challenges: "One immunizes the contents of the collective imagination by means of a small inoculation of acknowledged evil; one thus protects it against the risk of a generalized subversion" (140). Robert Lindner's treatise on psychopathy illustrates the process of inoculation at work in traditional criminology: "Psychological science has provided us with an instrument to study [the psychopath] closely and at first hand; to examine him thoroughly as we would a virulent bacillus; to dissect him and obtain his measure; perhaps even—assisted by those great social forces which are beginning to clear the slime and muck of underprivilege and economic expediency—to make of him a good citizen in a new world" (Lindner, *Rebel*, 16). In this passage, the possibility that the source of crime is located in the social structure is subordinated—both conceptually and syntactically—to the "real" problem of treating individual criminals.

Barthes takes an essentially rhetorical approach to evaluating the status of overtly resistant discourse; he examines not only what a text or myth claims to do but also how that text makes itself persuasive and what it is likely to persuade us to do. Viewed from this perspective, even the debate between biological and cultural determinism—a primary subtext for all five novels examined in the following pages—can be translated into a dialogue about the source of crime; the behavior of a culturally determined psychopath can be just as "determined" as that of a biologically determined one. In the dominant discourse, deterministic models—both biological and cultural—may be seen as alternative ways of understanding the mechanisms that produce dangerous individuals. The models need not effect changes in the way we treat those individuals or attempt to reduce crime. Rather than prompt us to do something different to reduce crime, they may help us do more of the same.

Statistics as well as anthropological investigations show us crime, then, as a natural phenomenon, a phenomenon . . . as necessary as birth, death, or conception.

At the sight of these strange anomalies the problem of the nature and of the origin of the criminal seemed to me resolved; the characteristics of primitive men and of inferior animals must be reproduced in our times.

—Cesare Lombroso

T W O

Frank Norris's *McTeague:* Darwin and Police Power

Naturalism may be defined as the application of determinism to a literary form. The naturalist novel typically relies on the conventions of realism to illustrate, in narrative, the operation of some force that determines human personality and behavior. If we approach literature using this definition, however, we allow the naturalists too much say in how their work is read. A writer may have intended a particular novel, for example, to illustrate Darwinism at work, but Darwinism, at least as it is publicly known, may be adapted or distorted to support an array of ideologies. Put simply, the deterministic forces in the lives of naturalist characters are not "natural" at all. Rather, they are myths that tell us more about culture and ideology than about the forces that shape human behavior.

One mythic version of Darwinism that flourished at the turn of the century centered on the concept of degeneration, or reversion. In the eugenics movement, and in the theories of the criminologist Cesare Lombroso and Max Nordau, Lombroso's most famous disciple, there arose the idea that the "natural" direction of evolution, which was toward progress and improvement, could be thwarted and even reversed under certain conditions. Lombroso used the concept of degeneration to provide a biological basis for his model of the "born criminal," an atavistic being condemned to a life of crime.

Lombroso's theories inform Frank Norris's *McTeague*[1] as well as the newspaper reports of the notorious San Francisco murder case that inspired the novel. On the morning of October 9, 1893, Patrick Collins murdered his wife in the hat room of the San Francisco kindergarten where she worked as a cleaning woman. Sarah Collins received more than thirty stab wounds. Perhaps because the crime was especially brutal, the local press covered the case extensively. Many details of plot, character, and setting in *McTeague* come directly from the reported details.[2]

One of the headlines in the first article to appear reads, "Sarah Collins Slaughtered By Her Husband Because She Would Not Give Him Money." Patrick Collins, it was said, had been a satisfactory husband at the beginning of the marriage, but as his alcoholism developed, he became brutal and disinclined to work. He eventually abandoned his wife, although he returned periodically to threaten her and to extort money. Sarah Collins, like McTeague's wife, Trina, was famous among her acquaintances for her extreme industry and thrift.

Newspaper coverage of the murder described Collins in terms that linked criminal attributes with animal ones. An article published in the *San Francisco Examiner* a few days after the murder, calls Collins "the savage of civilization" and a "human beast." This piece, under the headline "He was Born for the Rope," begins: "If a good many of Patrick Collins' ancestors did not die on the scaffold then either they escaped their desert or there is nothing in heredity." The writer stresses the role of deterministic biological forces again farther down the page: "[Collins's] face is not degraded, but brutish. That is to say,

---

[1] Donald Pizer documents some connections between *McTeague* and Lombroso in *The Novels of Frank Norris*. See also William B. Dillingham's *Frank Norris: Instinct and Art*.

[2] Two articles from the *San Francisco Examiner* are reprinted in the Norton Critical Edition of the novel.

he is not a man who has sunk, but one who was made an animal by nature to start with." One brief headline reads simply, "He is a Type."

In ascribing Collins's criminality to his animal nature and his brutishness, the *Examiner* articles echo Lombroso, who believed that "born criminals" made up about 40 percent of the criminal population. Born criminals, unlike others, manifested certain atavistic physical traits. These traits "prove clearly that the most horrible crimes have their origin in those animal instincts of which childhood is a pale reflection. Repressed in civilized man by education, environment, and the fear of punishment, they suddenly break out in the born criminal without apparent cause, or under the influence of certain circumstances, such as sickness, atmospheric influences, sexual excitement, or . . . chronic intoxication" (368). According to Lombroso, we must identify these defective beings and separate them from both society and other wrongdoers, because there is virtually no chance of rehabilitating them.

As science, the Lombrosian model has been discredited and largely forgotten, and even as a source for *McTeague* the subject might seem to have limited interest. Lombrosian criminology and its various manifestations, however, perform cultural work as artifacts by naturalizing socially constructed concepts of criminality and normalcy. Lombroso's theories legitimate a system for apprehending, examining, classifying, and punishing criminals by presenting that system as a kind of taxonomy.

Maurice Parmelee's introduction to Lombroso's *Crime: Its Causes and Remedies*, for example, claims that Lombroso found the precursors of both crime and punishment in the animal world: "Not only the equivalents of crime but those of punishment, also, have been noted among the lower species. Many cases are on record of a group of animals having torn to pieces one of its members who had committed an act contrary to the welfare of the group or had failed in performing its duties towards the group. In this blind act of vengeance we see the embryo of the form of social reaction called punishment" (xv). From the "blind act of vengeance," according to this reasoning, there evolved the modern criminal justice system, which does not create new human law but rather reflects and enhances the eternal laws of animal nature.

23

Lombroso's proposed model of punishment and incarceration has the ultimate aim of furthering "natural" selection. Lombroso suggests that incorrigible offenders, especially those exhibiting the physical traits of born criminals, should be confined by themselves in special penal institutions. "In this way [i.e., by establishing special penal institutions for born criminals] we shall apply anew to society the process of selection to which is due the existence of our race, and also probably the existence of justice itself, since it was the elimination of the more violent that gradually allowed justice to prevail" (Lombroso, 425). In its ideal form, then, the criminal justice system simply helps nature. Lombroso also extends the analogy to encompass execution: "when, in spite of the prison, transportation, and hard labor, these criminals repeat their sanguinary crimes and threaten the lives of honest men for the third or fourth time there is nothing left but the last selection, painful but sure,—capital punishment) . . . To claim that the death penalty is contrary to the laws of nature is to ignore the fact that this law is written in the book of nature in letters only too clear, and that the very progress of the organic world is entirely based upon the struggle for existence, followed by savage hecatombs" (426–27).

By reproducing fundamental elements of Lombrosian criminology in narrative form, *McTeague* participates in the naturalization of the power to incarcerate. The novel depicts police functions as extensions of natural law and endows socially constructed concepts of normalcy and criminality with a biological foundation. Norris manipulates theories of degeneracy to suggest that criminal delinquency is rooted in heredity, that criminality is a relic of our animal past, that incarceration and execution are forms of natural selection, and that the law-abiding worker is the culmination of millions of years of progressive evolution.

It is illuminating to compare newspaper coverage of the Collins murder to the finished novel. While many details survive unchanged in translation, there are some significant alterations. The police, the prison, and the gallows all figure prominently in the newspaper reports, for example, but play virtually no role in McTeague's life. Collins was arrested less than twenty-four hours after the murder, but McTeague eludes the police and escapes into the desert. Collins had previously served six months in jail, having been convicted of assaulting his wife, but McTeague has neither a criminal record nor prison experience. Collins was hanged; McTeague dies of deprivation in Death Valley. In adapting the Collins story for his novel, Norris eliminated all evidence of the criminal justice system—the police, the jail, and the rope.

These omissions might seem to exclude *McTeague* from a study of execution novels, but closer examination reveals that while Norris removed the agents of power, the effects of the power remain. *McTeague* is an execution novel without executioners. The novel deletes the historical and political context of the actual murder in a manner that recalls Barthes's description of the naturalizing function of myth. Norris sketches a diagram of the criminal justice system while allowing the system's mechanisms, officers, and institutions to remain invisible. We gaze upon McTeague with the same appraising stare that the criminal justice system turns on its wards. Our examination shows that McTeague, like Collins, succumbs to deterministic forces that he can neither resist nor understand. When the hulking dentist ventures onto the floor of Death Valley, he enters a natural Death Row, a region without shade, a region where he can be seen with absolute clarity. He is handcuffed and sentenced to death. We last see him as he awaits execution. The novel assures its readers that Lombroso has discovered, rather than invented, the born murderer.

Under natural law McTeague gets the same punishment that he would have received from a judge and jury in apparent confirmation of Lombroso's claim "that we are governed by silent laws, which never fall into desuetude and rule society much more surely than the laws inscribed in the codes" (369). Lombrosian criminology naturalizes penal power by suggesting that a strong police force and the criminal justice system implement progressive evolution by culling the weak and the flawed from society so that the race remains hardy and vigorous. *McTeague* contributes to the naturalizing process by depicting the forces of nature doing the work of the police. The novel is thus more than failed anthropology, more than the remnant of erroneous but well-intentioned nineteenth-century cosmology. It is a kind of fossil, the physical remains of the mythic foundations of carceral power.

The entanglement of Lombrosian criminology and systemic power is amply demonstrated by the manner in which *McTeague* makes evidence of deterministic environmental forces—which might shift the responsibility for crime away from the individual criminal and onto society—subordinate to heredity. "The study of the [environmental] causes of crime does not lessen the fatal influence to be assigned to the organic factor, which certainly amounts to 35% and possibly even 40%; the so-called causes of crime being often only the last determinants and the great strength of congenital impulsiveness the principal cause" (Lombroso, 376).

Lombrosian criminology does not deny that social and environmental forces can cause crime but instead portrays them as mere catalysts to the more powerful organic imperative. In fact, both Norris and Lombroso place the criminal in a richly textured social and biological context, as would a radical or historicist approach to crime. Rather than treat crime as a matter of individual moral failure, as a struggle between good and evil, they depict it as the inevitable product of deterministic forces. The radicalism of this approach, however, is illusory. In the end both Lombroso and Norris subordinate environmental factors to a biological model that, like traditional moralistic models, unequivocally locates the source of crime within the individual.

Under the Lombrosian model, evidence of deterministic forces producing crime thus tends to increase the responsibility of the individual offender: "The fact that there exist such beings as born criminals, organically fitted for evil, atavistic reproductions, not simply of savage men but even of the fiercest animals, far from making us more compassionate towards them, as has been maintained, steels us against all pity" (Lombroso, 427). Lombroso's view of the relationship between determinism and responsibility is echoed by Foucault: "The more psychologically determined an act is found to be, the more its author can be considered legally responsible. The more the act is, so to speak, gratuitous and undetermined, the more it will tend to be excused. A paradox, then: the legal freedom of a subject is proven by the fact that his act is seen to be necessary, determined; his lack of responsibility proven by the fact that his act is seen to be unnecessary" ("The Dangerous Individual," 140). This paradox exists because, under both the disciplinary and the Lombrosian models, criminal responsibility not only reflects guilt with respect to a specific offense but also gauges the likelihood of future wrongdoing. If the criminal act in question was in fact the product of deterministic forces, then it is destined to be repeated. Lombroso's born criminal is a biologically determined form of Foucault's delinquent or repeat offender. In both cases incarceration (or execution) is required, because the offender represents an eminent danger to public safety.

The novel's demonstration that McTeague is both a born murderer and born for the rope represents a remarkable about-face in the context of late nineteenth-century debates concerning capital punishment, criminal responsibility, and mental illness. At the time the prevailing interpretation of the M'Naghten rule held that any derangement of the mental faculties severe enough to merit acquittal on the basis of insanity would be so marked and so obvious that expert testimony would be unnecessary. Members of the medical and mental health communities increasingly attacked this interpretation, however, and it was tested in a number of widely publicized trials through the "irresistible impulse" argument, which held that people could be driven by mental illness to perform actions that they knew were wrong.

Most notorious, perhaps, was the 1881 trial of Charles Julius Guiteau, the assassin of President James Garfield. That Guiteau had killed Garfield was never in doubt, and the courtroom proceedings were devoted almost entirely to testimony from medical experts debating the applicability of the insanity defense. Through biographical and medical testimony the defense sought to portray Guiteau as a congenital lunatic. According to the defense, Guiteau knew that it was wrong to take a life, but because of his mental illness, he could not resist the impulse to kill. The prosecution countered by arguing that far from being legally insane Guiteau was merely an eccentric who had wasted his life on dissipation and immoral behavior. The fact that Guiteau could keep a job and support himself, the prosecution contended, was evidence enough of his sanity. Guiteau was duly executed. But the trial was one of the most sensational and widely publicized in the nation's history, and after months of press coverage, the language of the debate—involving terms like criminal responsibility, nature, nurture, moral insanity, and moral imbecility—passed into public parlance.

By the time *McTeague* was published, the irresistible impulse defense used by Guiteau's lawyers had evolved in a curious direction. That is, it had switched sides. The notion of congenital criminality like McTeague's generates in readers more antipathy than sympathy. If we do not immediately recognize this criminal nature as outright lunacy, then it ultimately appears more dangerous for having escaped detection. If someone is biologically destined to live as a criminal, there is no hope of rehabilitation—and little to be gained by improving the cultural environment and the education available to the "criminal classes."

Although no one followed Lombroso's suggestion and set up special prisons for born criminals, many of the ideas associated with Lombroso and with the eugenics movement made their way into law. In McTeague, Norris gave his readers a dangerous figure that could justify attempts to legislate eugenics for the first three decades of the twentieth century. Beginning with Indiana in 1907 and California in 1909, a number of states passed laws requiring or permitting the sterilization of "defectives" and individuals determined to have inherited a criminal nature. Eventually about half of the states enacted such legislation (Friedman, 336). Untold numbers of Americans, almost exclusively poor people and immigrants, eventually came under the knife. As late as 1927, when the Supreme Court upheld an involuntary sterilization law in *Buck v. Bell*, these laws enjoyed wide support and were grounded in the same logic that allowed Justice Oliver Wendell Holmes to write, in the majority opinion, that it was better to sterilize defectives and degenerates than to "execute [their] degenerate offspring for crime . . . Three generations of imbeciles are enough" (quoted in Friedman, 337).

By elaborating on the dangers associated with defective and degenerate blood, then, *McTeague* both reflects and participates in the exercise of police power. The novel assures us, using scientific evidence, that there is an enemy in our midst. We live with an atavistic subrace of individuals who look and speak like the rest of us but who may erupt at any time in murderous violence. These people endanger not only their particular victims but also the entire race. If they are allowed to live and breed like the rest of us, they will reduce humanity once again to savagery. Society has the responsibility of protecting itself by aggressively policing the line between criminal and normal. Norris thus follows Lombroso and Nordau in invoking spurious biology to sanction the expansion of correctional and police power. *McTeague* justifies capital punishment by proving that some people are murderers before they kill and by establishing the capital offender as a biologically determined human type. The scapegoat is thus hailed as a work of nature.

Lombroso's *Crime: Its Causes and Remedies* was first published in the United States as a part of the *Modern Criminal Science Series*, under the auspices of the American Institute of Criminal Law and Criminology. The series had its origins in a 1909 conference in Chicago and was intended to make the most important works of European criminologists readily available in English translations. Lombroso did not attend the conference (he was in poor health and died within the year), but he did write an encouraging letter to Professor John H. Wigmore, one of the organizers.

In his introduction to the English version of *Crime: Its Causes and Remedies*, Maurice Parmelee quotes the letter: "If I could offer any suggestion to so competent a body of men, it would be to emphasize the importance of apportioning penalties, not according to the offense, but according to the offender. . . . It is futile to fix a term of imprisonment for the born criminal; but it is necessary to shorten to the minimum the term for the emotional offender, and to modify it for the occasional offender, and to place the latter under the supervision of a judge, and not to let his fate be so fixed that it amounts merely to a modern form of slavery" (xiii). Lombroso calls for a systematic approach to identifying and classifying criminals; punishment must be individualized, and the process of individualization requires a scrupulous examination and diagnosis of each criminal.

The ultimate aim of such examinations is to separate the born criminals from those offenders with the potential to reform (Lombroso uses terms such as "criminaloid" to refer to borderline cases). One method requires the precise measurement of physical characteristics. Born criminals have one or more "atavistic" features, such as "enormous development of the maxillaries and the zygomata; prognathism . . . greater pigmentation of the skin; tufted and crispy hair; and large ears" (Lombroso, 365). Physically, McTeague seems drawn with such traits in mind. His head is "square-cut, angular; the jaw salient, like that of a carnivora" (7). Norris's descriptions emphasize the dentist's animal qualities: "altogether he suggested the draft horse, immensely strong, stupid, docile, obedient" (7).

Lombroso's other methods of identifying born criminals were technologically more sophisticated. He recommended, for example, the use of a "plethysmograph," which measured variations in the flow of blood. According to Lombroso, plethysmography offered a superior alternative to torture because it was both more reliable and a more humane way of eliciting the truth from the accused. By this means, Lombroso declared, one could "penetrate into the most secret recesses of the mind of the criminal" (254).

In addition to various physical clues, suspicious habits were often giveaways. The born criminal was biologically fated not only to commit crimes but also to engage in other compulsive, albeit legal, behaviors. The Lombrosian model equated physical characteristics, such as prognathism and crispy hair, with behavioral ones, such as tattooing or the obsessive collecting of material objects. Nordau commented on "the existence of an irresistible desire among the degenerate to accumulate useless trifles" (*Degeneration*, 27). McTeague's strange fondness for trinkets and shiny objects—Trina's tooth, the concertina, the canary in its cage, the "office effects" from his dental practice (213)—thus branded him as surely as did his physical appearance.

The ultimate proof of born criminality, however, came from diagnostic biography. In *Crime: Its Causes and Remedies*, Lombroso quoted Delbruck[3] on the search for the perpetrator of a crime: "Knowledge of the act . . . with an examination of the body and the mind before and after it, is not enough to clear up the question of responsibility; it is necessary to know the life of the criminal from the cradle to the dissecting table" (378). *McTeague*, like the criminal biography that Delbruck recommends, is a sort of narrative vivisection of a murderer, a criminal exposé that proceeds through a scrupulous examination of

---

[3] *Zeitschrift für Psychiatrie* (1864): 72.

the criminal's life and body. The conclusions reached by exercises in diagnostic biography express themselves in the form of personality types, and the designation of born criminal is justified by a biography that closely parallels an agreed-upon model. Anecdotes about early childhood experiences, domestic turbulence, and past behavior foreshadow later crimes. We see that the crime in question is just a revealing incident, an unmasking of the dangerous personality that was there, hidden, all along.

Diagnostic criminal biography is supposed to be faithful to an ideal of clinical detachment, but clearly such objectivity is hard to sustain and impossible to verify. The occasion for diagnosis is a criminal act, and in the case of capital crimes the act is so reprehensible that it colors all biographical detail. Everything learned about the offender's life may seem to culminate in one desperate moment. The pretense of objectivity obscures this revisionist aspect, so that the offender's assignment to a particular criminal type appears to be no more than diagnosis.

McTeague obscures its revisionist origins in part by inverting the narrative chronology of the biographies on which the novel is based. Norris's starting point was a newspaper article about a woman found murdered in a kindergarten. Like the official investigators and the reporters who covered the story, Norris probed the killer's past to understand the crime, but his novel reverses the chronological sequence, beginning long before the crime and proceeding toward it. As a result McTeague appears all the more to have been born a criminal, his life shaped by deterministic forces that proceed inexorably before the readers' eyes.

The biographical search for the origins of criminality designates any abnormal or deviant behavior as precriminal. Consequently this search can be said to define the limits of normality. Normalizing judgment, far from being limited to statutory matters, labels all behavior either normal or abnormal, as forbidden or condoned. The Lombrosian concept of degeneration naturalizes this normalizing judgment by linking both normality and abnormality to heredity.

In his introduction to the 1968 edition of Max Nordau's *Degeneration*, George L. Mosse notes that Nordau proposed an organic basis for a morality that is "identical with commonly accepted middle-class morality. Those who do not share such a morality must be examined for signs of degeneracy" (xxiv). His book attacked the various nontraditional approaches to art that became modernism. Nordau adopted the stance of a conservative skeptic battling the immorality, decadence, mysticism, and irrationality that threatened to overwhelm society. In the first chapter, "Fin-de-Siècle," he listed several examples of so-called *fin-de-siècle* consciousness and argued that they have only one connection: "a contempt for traditional views of custom and morality" (5). Degeneration he defined as a "morbid deviation from an original type" (Nordau, 16). The original type achieved full flower in middle-class standards of normalcy.

One particularly interesting aspect of the theme of organic normalcy is the suggestion that healthy humans have an instinct for police work. Nordau described—in terms that echo Norris's novel—the form that such instinctive policing might take:

> Whoever believes with me that society is the natural organic form of humanity, in which alone it can exist, prosper, and continue to develop itself to higher destinies . . . must mercilessly crush under his thumb the antisocial vermin. To him who, with Nietzsche, is enthusiastic over the "freely-roving, lusting beast of prey," we cry, "Get you gone from civilization! Rove far from us! Be a lusting beast of prey in the desert! . . . Our streets and our houses are not built for you; our looms have no stuffs for you; our fields are not tilled for you. All our labour is performed by men who esteem each other, have consideration for each other, mutually aid each other, and know how to curb their selfishness for the general good. There is no place among us for the lusting beast of prey; and if you dare return to us, we will pitilessly beat you to death with clubs." (557)

To Nordau, the official police force is merely an organized version of these good men with clubs.

McTeague has police functions performed by natural or "amateur" agents.[4] As I have noted, this naturalization process includes the equation of police actions with natural selection. The born criminal proves simply too weak to compete with stronger, normal, law-abiding citizens. Nordau claimed that degenerates "can neither adapt

---

[4] I have appropriated the use of "amateur" in this context from D. A. Miller.

themselves to the conditions of nature and civilization, nor maintain themselves in the struggle for existence against the healthy" (541). Note, for example, that when Zerkow kills Maria, the police are confident that he will quickly be captured. Instead his body is found floating in the bay. At least in the novel, the murderer's death seems to follow naturally from his crime. Norris also naturalizes police functions, as Nordau did, by suggesting that police work is a normal human instinct. The agent of McTeague's punishment is not a police officer but Trina's cousin. Against improbable odds, Marcus tracks McTeague to Death Valley and dispenses justice. McTeague ends up handcuffed, in custody, and sentenced to death, just as he would have been if the police had intervened.

Marcus's status as an amateur police agent is enhanced by the fact that he twice has the occasion to act as a deputy sheriff. At one point he spends a violent week as a deputy helping to quell a strike in Sacramento. Just before the novel's end, too, he rides with a deputized posse that is hunting McTeague. The sheriff leading the posse refuses to chase McTeague into Death Valley, but Marcus is able to break from the group because "in the haste of the departure from Keeler the sheriff had neglected to swear him in. He was under no orders" (334). Marcus remains an amateur agent, but the novel encourages readers to identify Marcus with the police. The criminal justice system thus merges with the other, more "natural" forces that govern Marcus's behavior: family ties, revenge, and greed. In a world where normal adults instinctively police and punish, the criminal stands no chance of success.

The novel further reinforces middle-class norms by suggesting that the urge to work and save money is instinctual. As Trina degenerates, she develops certain manias, certain obsessions—in short, Trina becomes a parody of the ideal worker. McTeague eventually despises her for her "excessive industry" and because she is so "invariably correct and precise." She labors every spare minute for subsistence wages. The money she does manage to save is invested in her uncle's business. At one point McTeague threatens to beat her if she doesn't quit working in front of him (237).

Trina is eventually reduced to a machinelike existence: "Trina's emotions had narrowed with the narrowing of her daily life. They reduced themselves at last to but two, her passion for her money and her perverted love for her husband when he was brutal. She was a strange woman during these days" (239). Trina's drive to work and save is as fundamental to her as her sexual instinct, and eventually the two drives merge: "She had her money, that was the main thing. Her passion for it excluded every other sentiment. . . . Not a day passed that Trina did not have it out where she could see it and touch it. One evening she had even spread all the gold pieces between the sheets, and had then gone to bed, stripping herself, and had slept all night upon the money, taking a strange and ecstatic pleasure in the touch of the smooth flat pieces the length of her entire body" (277).

Even McTeague has some "instincts" that make him especially well suited for work in a disciplinary society. He readily adapts to life at the mine, even though it is a life of unremitting toil and deprivation. He works twelve hours each day and spends the remaining twelve eating or sleeping in a barracks. Despite the monotonous routine, this "life pleased the dentist beyond words" (298). McTeague adapts easily to mining work perhaps because he has returned to the place and the life to which he was born: "straight as a homing pigeon and following a blind and unreasoned instinct, McTeague had returned to the Big Dipper mine. Within a week's time it seemed to him as if he had never been away" (297). The novel establishes a biologically determined norm, both for individuals and for society. For McTeague the norm is a life of unrelenting, mind-numbing toil.

A biologically determined model of normalcy also controls much of the novel's plot. The action moves from disrupted natural state to the restoration of order. As the novel opens, McTeague is living above his station: he is a laborer posing as a member of the professional class without the sanction of blood or education. He seems even more out of place when his wife wins the lottery. Because they are not of a moneyed class, McTeague and Trina do not know how to manage money properly, as, for example, Uncle Oelbermann does. Once McTeague's dental practice has been suspended, he depends on Trina for money, a role reversal that disrupts the "natural" power relationship between man and wife. Consider, for example, the dialogue as McTeague confronts Trina about her decision to rent a cheaper apartment:

34

"Are you my boss, I'd like to know? Who's the boss, you or I?"

"Who's got the *money*, I'd like to know?" cried Trina, flushing to her pale lips. "Answer me that, McTeague, who's got the money?" [211]

The violations of propriety cumulatively create enough stress to force McTeague's true character to exert itself. Once he stands revealed as a born criminal, the plot shifts toward a restoration of the natural order. When McTeague degenerates, he slides down the social ladder and eventually dies. The implication is that, given time people will rise or sink to their proper, biologically determined stations, with or without the help of the police, and that society will thereafter regain its balance.

The exercise of institutional power depends upon a politics of vision. Diagnostic biography posits the existence of a trained eye that is capable of seeing into the criminal's soul and does not blink before coercive normalization of the noncriminal. Such politicized vision is readily conceivable in a prison. But how can it be institutionalized in open society? We must remember, first, that surveillance may be either actual or imagined. For an example of the imaginary observing gaze, recall the inmates of Bentham's Panopticon, who could never be sure if anyone was in the observation tower. To accommodate the uncertainty, they internalized the observing eye and behaved as if they were always being watched.

Thomas Byrnes's *Professional Criminals of America* (1886) sets forth one strategy for extending symbolic surveillance beyond prison walls. Byrnes was chief of detectives in the New York City Police Department, and his book included photographs and brief profiles of 247 known criminals in the hope that they might be recognized and apprehended. In the preface he writes: "It is my belief that if men and women who make a practice of preying upon society were known to others besides detectives and frequenters of the courts, a check, if not a complete stop, would be put to their exploits. While the photographs of burglars, forgers, sneak thieves, and robbers of lesser degree are kept in police albums, many offenders are still able to operate successfully. But with their likenesses within reach of all, their vocation would soon become risky and unprofitable" (n.p.). Byrnes proposes universal surveillance, to be implemented by an informed populace. The 247 criminals portrayed in his book would find themselves thrust under a virtually omniscient gaze as more and more civilians were recruited to police work. Because these amateur police agents could not readily be identified, the criminals on Byrnes's list would risk capture every time they appeared in public. Byrnes felt that the project would lead to the arrest of at least some of his subjects, but he also hoped for a more significant result: criminals would abandon crime when they perceived its futility.

Norris makes a similar connection between an imagined omniscient gaze and police work. In "A Plea for Romantic Fiction," he describes a personified version of romance. Characterized in terms that recall the crime and police literature of the day, Norris's Romance combines the skills of the trained detective with the interpretive powers of the natural historian: "So you think Romance would stop in the front parlour and discuss medicated flannels and mineral water with the ladies? Not for more than five minutes. She would be off upstairs with you, prying, peeping, peering into the closets of the bedroom, into the nursery, into the sitting room; yes, and into that little iron box screwed to the lower shelf of the closet in the library; and into those compartments and pigeonholes of the *secrétaire* in the study" (*Complete Works*, VII, 165–66). Norris's Romance sees into people's homes and ferrets out the clues that reveal their hopes, their hidden crimes, and their "secretest life" (165).

McTeague engages in its own version of this romantic prying by looking into the apartments of the citizens of Polk Street and uncovering their secret lives. The novel's omniscient narrator places the characters under surveillance, envisioning McTeague's apartment building as a sort of panopticon and the individual rooms of the flat as open-sided cells. A seemingly normal working-class neighborhood is revealed as a hiding place for born criminals and degenerates. The heightened vision of the narrator allows us to see that the local dentist and the "rags-bottles-sacks man" are murderers and that the women they marry are atavistic counterfeits of modern humans.

The narrative vision of the novel also resembles surveillance. It authoritatively detects and correctly interprets material and psychological details large and small. For example, the first chapter of *McTeague* ends rather abruptly when Marcus speaks the following words: "Say,

Mac, I told my cousin Trina to come round and see you about that tooth of hers. She'll be in tomorrow, I guess" (15). This remark seems insignificant as we read it, but in the narrator's panoptic vision, this statement marks the moment that decides the fate of all three characters—as we later realize.

The narrator sees through physical barriers, into the future, and into the minds of most characters, a feat that is the narrative equivalent of Lombroso's vaunted plethysmography. Norris seems to have considered the ability to see through lies and public facades a characteristic of romance. In "A Plea for Romantic Fiction," he calls romance "an instrument keen, finely tempered, flawless—an instrument with which we may go straight through the clothes and tissues and wrappings of flesh down deep into the red, living heart of things" (*Complete Works*, VII, 163). Using this "instrument keen," *McTeague*'s narrator sees the personalities of the novel's characters more clearly than they do. When McTeague kisses Trina for the first time, for example, the narrator anticipates McTeague's rejection and ultimate murder of his wife: "The instant that Trina gave up, the instant she allowed him to kiss her, he thought less of her. She was not so desirable after all. But this reaction was so faint, so subtle, so intangible, that in another moment he had doubted its occurrence" (69–70).

McTeague may doubt that this change has occurred, but the reader cannot. In fact, the novel has already anticipated McTeague's violent transformation when, while treating Trina's broken tooth, McTeague first becomes sexually aware. "His whole rude idea of life had to be changed. The male, virile desire in him tardily awakened, aroused itself, strong and brutal. It was resistless, untrained, a thing not be held in leash an instant" (25). McTeague's newly awakened self, which is brutal and resists restraint, marks him as a criminal and a future murderer. Trina is likewise subjected to the narrator's scrutiny. When McTeague embraces her, causing the "woman" to be born within the girl, the narrator sees more than Trina can: "Dimly, as figures seen in a waking dream, these ideas floated through Trina's mind. It was quite beyond her to realize them clearly; she could not know what they meant" (73).

The heightened vision of the narrator shows that most of the novel's central characters have dual personalities. We first see Mc-

Teague's dual self when he stands over Trina's anesthesized body. On the one side, we see McTeague's superficial goodness and, on the other, his congenital evil: "Within him, a certain second self, another better McTeague rose with the brute; both were strong, with the huge, crude strength of the man himself. . . . There in that cheap and shabby Dental Parlors a dreaded struggle began. It was the old battle, old as the world, wide as the world—the sudden panther leap of the animal, lips drawn, fangs aflash, hideous, monstrous, not to be resisted, and the simultaneous arousing of the other man, the better self that cries, 'Down, down,' without knowing why; that grips the monster; that fights to strangle it, to thrust it down and back" (28). Eventually, McTeague gives in to the "foul stream of hereditary evil" that runs within him (29) and kisses the unconscious Trina "grossly, full on the mouth" (28).

The novel casts McTeague as a degenerate, as a human who has reverted to his animal origins, but the dichotomies that inform this image of degeneracy parallel those inherent in a system of corrective surveillance. The novel's image of the divided self corresponds to human identity with its animal and moral aspects, but the divided self also mirrors the split personality produced by the technologies of surveillance: one self has criminal desires that are held in check by the policing tendencies of the other. McTeague, a prisoner of the panopticon, struggles between what he would do if he were being watched and what he would do if he were not. Trina's gaze restrains McTeague; he does not lose control of himself until she is unconscious.

The dual self motif illustrates another aspect of surveillance as well when Marcus renounced his "claims" on Trina. Whereas McTeague acts because he suddenly finds himself unobserved, Marcus's actions respond to the promptings of an imaginary audience. He "saw himself as another man, very noble, self-sacrificing; he stood apart and watched this second self with boundless admiration and with infinite pity" (48). Marcus imagines himself onstage, and the passage shows how self-surveillance becomes a mechanism for the construction of the self. McTeague embodies both release and restraint; he has a sexual self and an asexual self. Marcus, on the other hand, is both the audience and the starring performer in a play of his own devising.

38

Even when Marcus imagines how an audience might see him, of course, he cannot see himself as the narrator does. The reader, who has access to the narrator's vision, sees Marcus making himself ridiculous. During one scene in the novel, however, a character briefly looks through the narrator's eyes. Trina comes upon McTeague one Sunday afternoon, three weeks after their marriage, as he sleeps in his dental chair. Trina, startled, sees her husband as if for the first time:

> Her husband was in the Dental Parlors, lying back in his operating chair, fast asleep. The little stove was crammed with coke; the room was overheated, the air thick and foul with the odors of ether, of coke gas, of stale beer and cheap tobacco. The dentist sprawled his gigantic limbs over the worn velvet of the operating chair; his coat and vest and shoes were off, and his huge feet, in their thick grey socks, dangled over the edge of the footrest; his pipe, fallen from his half-open mouth, had spilled the ashes into his lap; while on the floor, at his side, stood the half-empty pitcher of steam beer. His head had rolled limply upon one shoulder, his face was red with sleep, and from his open mouth came a terrific sound of snoring. [145–46]

Trina stares at this scene for a moment, then runs sobbing to her bed, suddenly aware that her marriage was a "dreadful mistake." As if for the first time, she notices McTeague's "salient jaw" and his "elephantine" feet (146). Trina momentarily sees McTeague as the reader does in the novel's opening scenes, which also depict the dentist's regular Sunday afternoon nap. Asleep in the operating chair, McTeague, now himself the "anesthesized" patient who is unable to see but is observed by a clinical, all-seeing eye, functions as an analog for the inmate in the panopticon, while Trina temporarily sees with the eyes of the diagnostician. As soon as McTeague is awake, Trina's "realistic" vision evaporates.

Trina's moment of privileged vision is not repeated, but the scene does provide a prototype for a number of other scenes in which the narrator describes characters unaware of being observed. Just as the prison cell produces precise diagnostic information about the inmate, these scenes of imagined privacy generate privileged information about character. The behavior of the individual in a completely pri-

vate setting illustrates, by contrast, the specific ways in which surveillance shapes behavior. These scenes place characters figuratively as
well as literally in the operating chair. Unconscious of our observing
presence, they reveal their true selves.

One such scene involving Marcus occurs on the night of Trina's
lottery win. Marcus, who has remained strangely silent throughout
the evening's festivities, leaves his companions to check on the dogs
in his care:

> For the first time that evening he was alone and could give vent to his
> thoughts. He took a couple of turns up and down the yard, then suddenly
> in a low voice exclaimed, "You fool, you fool, Marcus Schouler! If you'd
> kept Trina you'd have had that money. . . . You've thrown away your
> chance in life—to give up the girl, yes—but this"—he stamped his foot
> with rage—"to throw five thousand dollars out of the window—to stuff it
> into the pockets of someone else when it might have been yours, when
> you might have had Trina *and* the money—and all for what? Because we
> were pals. Oh, pals is all right—but five thousand dollars—to have played
> it right into his hands—God damn the luck!" [103]

This scene shows how surveillance facilitates diagnoses and also illustrates how Marcus has been affected by what other people think.
Marcus's outburst confirms our suspicions that his noble speeches
about friendship serve only to disguise his true motives. Like a similar
scene in which McTeague spends the night alone in Trina's room (64–
66), this scene shows how the novel exposes a character's true
thoughts and motives.

Scenes of imagined privacy reinforce our sense that the narrator is
both objective and omniscient; the narrator, invisible to the characters, sees through shams, lies, and masquerades and consistently reveals the "truths" of human behavior. The objective truth of the narrative vision is also confirmed through the novelistic equivalent of
control groups. *McTeague* tells the stories of three romances, all of
which lead to weddings. Norris is charting the actions of deterministic forces that should theoretically affect the three stories in similar
ways.

The "romance" between Zerkow and Maria, for example, presents
a more advanced form of the degeneracy and congenital atavism that

dooms McTeague and Trina. Maria and Trina are both stingy and in-dustrious, and both develop obsessions with gold. As Trina deterio-rates, she becomes increasingly friendly with Maria, and eventually replaces her—literally when she moves into Maria's former hovel and figuratively when she becomes deranged like Maria. Likewise, Mc-Teague replaces Zerkow, moving into the hovel, becoming obsessed with his own wife's gold, and eventually, like Zerkow, murdering her for it. On Norris's map of the forces that shape human lives, the two couples differ only in that one starts down the path of degeneracy before the other.

Grannis and Miss Baker, however, represent something entirely different. It may be going too far to say that they are idealized—they are, after all, somewhat pathetic figures—but the survival of their marriage indicates that they have succeeded in some way. Obviously, these two have not degenerated like many of the novel's other char-acters. Part of the reason may lie in their rather vague connections to a higher social class; in contrast, McTeague was only rather tenuously connected to a social class higher than the one into which he was born. Certainly Grannis and Miss Baker do not exhibit the physical signs of degeneracy seen in the other couples. Then, too, of all the characters in the novel, these two seem to have most internalized the panoptic gaze. When we see them alone in their rooms, we see not wild-eyed anger or mental disease but meticulous propriety. They are both in the habit of leaving their doors slightly open, as if to permit observation. Their awareness that the sounds they make are being interpreted prompts them to develop a sort of communication through mutual surveillance. No one in the novel is more timid, more aware of the dangers of social blundering, or quicker to blush. This quality of self-policing distinguishes Grannis and Miss Baker from the others, and it also shows how the trained eye of diagnostic vision can enforce norms.

If Grannis and Miss Baker represent a "healthful" internalization of the panoptic gaze, McTeague illustrates a more pathological model. After Trina's murder, McTeague develops a paranoid streak and be-lieves that he is being watched. Norris suggests that stress helps re-veal McTeague's animalistic personality. Again, however, McTeague's transformation is described in terms reminiscent of surveillance; like the inmates of Bentham's prison, McTeague internalizes a panoptic gaze and one that, furthermore, is explicitly linked to the police. When McTeague leaves the mine, he does so two days ahead of the "sheriff of Placer County and the two deputies from San Francisco" (301). McTeague's internalized watchful eye is a sort of self-policing mechanism that eventually impels him to carry out his own death sentence.

McTeague exhibits paranoia in the final chapters of the novel, but this is not the only time that he has believed himself watched by some powerful but invisible eye. A similar feeling grips McTeague and Trina after they receive the first letter from City Hall requiring McTeague to quit his dental practice because he lacks the proper credentials. From the time McTeague sees the fat, official-looking envelope drop through his mail slot, his life is transformed. He and Trina struggle with the havoc wrought by a single, anonymous letter. How will City Hall even know whether or not McTeague suspends his practice? Eventually, hoping that no one will notice, hoping that no one is watching them, they decide to ignore the letter and to keep its existence a secret. McTeague continues his practice, but now he and his wife live in constant fear: "They heard no more from the City Hall, but the suspense of the situation was harrowing. . . . The terror of the thing was ever at their elbows, going to bed with them, sitting down with them at breakfast in the kitchen, keeping them company all through the day" (205). Now that they have entered the searchlight, they cannot escape it: "They'll arrest you. You'll go to prison" (203).

I do not mean to suggest that the novel's all-seeing force for order colludes with carceral power. It is conceivable, for example, that Norris mistakenly chose to naturalize a branch of criminology that would soon be discredited. It cannot be argued, however, that the use of Lombrosian criminology and its various manifestations amounted to innocent scientific error. Like the "eye" of City Hall, the novel's narrator sees every movement on Polk Street, indoors or out. The two observing eyes are also (revealingly) sensitive to issues of class. The gaze from City Hall protects professionals from having to compete with working-class imposters; in the novel, the narrator's scrutiny is reserved for the lower classes.

The narrative vision seems curiously deferential and myopic with regard to the upper classes. About Uncle Oelbermann, the narrator is strangely silent. Uncle Oelbermann is a well-heeled, successful businessman, and the people of Polk Street, like the narrator, find him inscrutable; the inmates cannot peer into the observation tower. At the wedding, everyone defers to Uncle Oelbermann, but he remains a figure of mystery and authority. Without even speaking, he "superintended Heise opening the case of champagne with the gravity of a magistrate" (132).

The novel's tendency to honor class differences is also evident from the few other scenes in which McTeague comes into contact with the upper classes. When McTeague goes with Marcus to pick up a dog from "the avenue," the nearby neighborhood of the wealthy, McTeague finds the dog owner's house as imposing and impenetrable as he will later find Uncle Oelbermann: "It was a huge mansionlike place, set in an enormous garden that occupied a whole third of the block; and while Marcus tramped up the front steps and rang the doorbell boldly, to show his independence, McTeague remained below on the sidewalk, gazing stupidly at the curtained windows, the marble steps, and the bronze griffins, troubled and a little confused by all this massive luxury" (13–14). McTeague, who acts deferentially, as if he is being watched, is unable to see into the house.[5] The curtained windows remind us that the windows on Polk Street have no blinds—or at least they do not shut out the narrator.

McTeague's nervousness in this scene can be traced to the curtained windows and to the possibility that some highly placed individual might catch him in an impropriety. For someone of McTeague's questionable social stature—is he a doctor or a merchant or a laborer?—the hierarchical gaze of surveillance is especially nerve-wracking. The same anxiety is apparent in the shop girls and apprentices, who are similarly situated between the rungs of the social ladder. On a night out at the theater, these groups are intensely aware of being observed: "At an unguarded moment they might be taken

---

[5] It is worth noting that when Norris's family first moved to San Francisco, they lived in a mansion on a street two blocks over from Polk Street (*Complete Works*, 7:xviii).

for toughs, so they generally erred in the other direction and were absurdly formal. No people have a keener eye for the amenities than those whose social position is not assured" (76).

Fearful of being regarded as "toughs" or members of the criminal class, these citizens of Polk Street believe all aspects of their lives and behavior to be surveillance. Their anxieties recall Foucault's contention that, as disciplinary forces become dissociated from the actual criminal justice system and disperse throughout a society, the corrective and diagnostic gaze of surveillance extends to all behavior. In addition to detecting and deterring specific crimes, surveillance subjects all behavior to judgment. All behavior is either good or bad, appropriate or inappropriate. The situation is especially confusing for the citizens of Polk Street: "There were certain limits which its dwellers could not overstep; but unfortunately for them, these limits were poorly defined" (76). Vaguely aware of an omniscient, judgmental eye, these citizens dissociate themselves from criminalized forms of dress, speech, and behavior. In this way they are normalized.

McTeague mirrors and participates in the discourse of penal power by extending biological determinism to encompass both the capital offender and the normal, working adult. In the world of the novel, humans' most fundamental aspect is their animal nature, which antedates civilization, is relatively free from historical or social forces, and is inherently criminal. According to this view, carceral power is rendered necessary by human nature. The novel conflates animal traits with criminal, links incarceration to natural selection, and establishes in the process that not all people are truly human and that true humans can extirpate animals like McTeague. In *McTeague*, the criminal justice system, a force indispensable for progressive evolution, is a mechanism for separating the civilized human from the savage.

Mr Savage tells the court that if these boys are hanged there will be no more boys like these.

—Clarence Darrow pleading for mercy for Nathan Leopold and Richard Loeb

Tens of thousands of men live in a comparatively easy environment and pass their lives as useful citizens with no taint of criminality to their names, who under a hard environment would be found in prison. . . . Heredity has everything to do with making the machine strong and capable, or weak and useless; but when the machine is made and thrown on the world in its imperfect shape, environment has everything to do in determining what its shape shall be.

—Clarence Darrow, *Crime: Its Cause and Treatment*

THREE

Theodore Dreiser's *An American Tragedy:* Resistance, Normalization, and Deterrence

Twenty-six years after the publication of Frank Norris's *McTeague*, Theodore Dreiser published *An American Tragedy*, a novel likewise inspired by a well-publicized capital murder case. Dreiser's real-life subject was Chester Gillette, a young man executed by the state of New York in 1908 for the murder by drowning of Grace "Billie" Brown. Gillette came from a poor family and had supported himself by doing odd jobs and menial labor for six years after his parents abandoned him at fourteen. He eventually found work in a factory owned by a wealthy uncle, and although his position and pay were modest, the family connection allowed him some social contact with high society.

At the time of the murder, Grace Brown, a secretary at the Gillette factory, was pregnant with Gillette's child, and he apparently planned the murder as a way of avoiding scandal and an undesirable marriage.

After persuading Brown to elope with him in upstate New York, Gillette carried out his plan. Gillette took Brown for a ride in a rowboat on Big Moose Lake and then threw her from the boat. Her face, arms, and hands were bruised and lacerated, and authorities concluded that she had been beaten with a tennis racket that Gillette took along on the outing. Gillette, who had been traveling under an assumed name, soon registered at a nearby hotel, perhaps believing that he would be presumed drowned and that his crime would go undiscovered. He was arrested within hours but contended to the last that Grace Brown had committed suicide after he refused to marry her.

For a few months in the summer of 1906, the trial was a sensation, at least in the regional press. Gillette proved a photogenic murderer, and the newspapers reported that the crowds attending his trial included numerous young female supporters. From jail he sold dozens of autographed photos of himself for five dollars apiece. The proceeds paid for catered meals that were served in his cell. Newspaper accounts stressed Gillette's utter lack of remorse. A disturbing self-portrait emerged even from his own account of Grace Brown's death. Gillette, himself a strong swimmer, stated that he had watched Brown drown from a few feet away without attempting to help her. His heartlessness fueled interest, as did his connection to one of the region's most wealthy families, but after his electrocution on March 30, 1908, the case received little attention. Sixteen years later, when Dreiser retold the story in a novel of more than eight hundred pages, he was reconstructing an obscure chapter in the history of capital punishment.

The novel's dependence on the Chester Gillette murder trial for plot, character, and circumstance is well documented. Dreiser's retelling, however, raises many questions about criminal responsibility and irresistible impulse that did not figure in the Gillette case.[1] Criminal

---

[1]Detailed accounts of the composition of *An American Tragedy* can be found

responsibility and irresistible impulse did stand at the very center of two far more sensational murder trials from the period. These other proceedings, because of their spectacular notoriety, shaped the public debate over the death penalty in the early decades of the century.

Both cases involved extremely wealthy defendants who were guilty by all accounts. Both received tremendous publicity and trials prolonged by well-financed, aggressive defense strategies. In the first, in 1906, millionaire Harry K. Thaw was found innocent by reason of insanity of the murder of architect Stanford White. In the second trial, which unfolded in 1924 as Dreiser was writing *An American Tragedy*, Nathan Leopold and Richard Loeb avoided the death penalty and were sentenced to "life plus ninety-nine years" after pleading guilty to the premeditated kidnapping and murder of fourteen-year-old Robert Franks.

The outcome was widely criticized in both cases, and protests voiced many of the same arguments against capital punishment that surface in Dreiser's novel and, much later, in the U.S. Supreme Court's majority opinion in *Furman v. Georgia*. In 1926, Dreiser's readers did not need to be reminded that the very wealthy could dodge the death penalty. Clyde Griffiths, bewildered, a child of poverty and a puppet of deterministic forces that he could not understand, contrasted starkly with the arrogance and willfulness of wealthy, cold-blooded murderers like Leopold, Loeb, and Thaw. As Dreiser's readers followed Clyde to the threshold of the death chamber, they would likely know that Leopold and Loeb were living in prison like exiled kings and that Harry Thaw was squandering inherited millions on a tour of European capitals.

Like *McTeague*, *An American Tragedy* has often been described as an exercise in objective realism. One early reviewer contended that Dreiser had written his book "with no thesis whatever, with no ulterior purpose beyond the complete uncovering of all the intricate network of causes which led to the event." This same reviewer argued that such scrupulous objectivity represented a dramatic change from Dreiser's earlier work: "Mr. Dreiser has changed both his method and his

---

in Robert Elias's *Theodore Dreiser: Apostle of Nature,* Ellen Moers's *Two Dreiser's,* and Donald Pizer's *The Novels of Theodore Dreiser: A Critical Study.*

point of view. He has withdrawn to a position of far more complete artistic 'detachment.' He gives me now for the first time an impression of 'impersonality,' 'objectivity,' 'impartiality.' He appears to me now for the first time in his fiction to be seeking sincerely and pretty successfully to tell the truth, all the relevant truth and nothing but the truth—and with such proportion and emphasis that every interest involved shall feel itself adequately represented" (Sherman, 21).

Another reviewer considered the novel so scientifically accurate that it constituted a kind of criminological treatise: "No one can question either the ring of truth in the incidents or the adequacy of the motives assigned. Thus and for these reasons are murders done" (Krutch, 10–11). Clarence Darrow, who as the nation's most famous trial lawyer had kept Leopold and Loeb from hanging, praised the book for its meticulous accuracy and realism. He wrote, "Dreiser carries the story straight, honest and true to its inevitable end" (9).

If there are superficial similarities between Norris's project and Dreiser's, however, there are also very important differences. Each novel creates an aura of disinterested scientific inquiry, but in their representations of capital murder and capital punishment, the two are rhetorically opposed. Norris's account of hereditary degeneracy and congenital criminality strengthens the state's case for execution and reinforces the dominant discourse. To allow McTeague to live would be to risk more murders and the continuance of his degenerate line. Dreiser counters *McTeague* with a narrative apparently designed to refute the dominant discourse and to undermine the state's case for execution. Clyde may have murdered—the novel is vague on this point—but he was certainly not biologically destined to murder. The forces that shaped Clyde's life are located not in his body but in his environment, and under different circumstances he might have become a law-abiding citizen.

As if to emphasize that Clyde's fate was not preordained, several incidents show that the course of Clyde's life was profoundly shaped by unlikely and arbitrary circumstance. The automobile accident in Kansas City forces Clyde to live the life of a fugitive while still an impressionable teenager. The chance meeting with the uncle he had never known brings him to Lycurgus, where he finds himself supervising the department in which Roberta works. The two are attracted

48

to one another from their first meeting, but the fatal affair begins only after a chance encounter at a local lake. Another unlikely encounter marks the beginning of Clyde's affair with Sondra Finchley; Sondra offers Clyde a ride because she mistakes him for his cousin Gilbert. Without this unlikely chain of coincidences, Clyde's life would not end in the electric chair.

By emphasizing the role of chance in Clyde's life, Dreiser undermines important elements of the typical diagnostic biography of an executable offender. Chance, however, forms but one part of the novel's resistant strategy. Dreiser's response to Gillette's crime is also shaped by the debate, which reached fever pitch in the 1920s, between environmental and biological determinists. As we saw in the previous chapter, *McTeague* endorses and naturalizes the tenets of biological determinism in a way that promotes the criminal justice system's power. By demonstrating that McTeague's murderous nature is congenital, the novel asserts that McTeague will always be dangerous regardless of his environment. In the world of *McTeague*, biological forces determine criminality, carceral power, and class divisions.

Dreiser's Clyde Griffiths, in contrast, appears to have no inherent, biological nature. Rather his identity reflects his experience and his immediate social environment. Unlike McTeague, Clyde is not constitutionally unsuited for life among the upper class. In the world of *An American Tragedy*, class divisions are accidents of birth rather than expressions of biological plan. The ultimate source of McTeague's murderous nature may lie within him, but the ultimate source of Clyde's desire to kill Roberta lies in the interaction of social pressures, unconscious motives, and sheer chance. From various strands of environmental determinism—including the Marxist critique of social class, the Freudian paradigm of human behavior and personality, and Boasian cultural determinism—Dreiser weaves a resistant discourse.

Dreiser's use of environmental determinism to plot a resistant strategy complements the novel's detailed critique of the criminal justice system. When Norris reconstructs the Collins case, he removes all evidence of the criminal justice system and creates a fable of biological destiny. In contrast, Dreiser devotes roughly a third of his novel to examining the criminal justice system's response to Roberta's death. He finds a system rife with bias and corruption and

49

swayed by the influence of money, social class, personal prejudice, and inflammatory press coverage. The judge and the lawyers for both sides view the trial as an opportunity for political gain, and the press sensationalizes the case for profit. The judicial ritual that culminates in Clyde's execution stands revealed as both arbitrary and corrupt.

Dreiser seems especially alert to diagnosis as it is used to identify executable offenders. Norris's novel minimizes the pitfalls of diagnosis; an omniscient, clinically detached narrator finds McTeague to be a born murderer in the same way that a naturalist distinguishes a toad from a frog. Dreiser takes the opposite approach. He introduces so many variables and so many opportunities for error that diagnosis seems hopelessly complicated. The narratives of Roberta's death presented at Clyde's trial prove inadequate, and even willfully inaccurate, when compared to the one produced by the novel's narrator, and even the narrator's version highlights the ambiguities of the case. Dreiser's reader knows that Clyde kills for reasons both more complex and more elusive than those specified at the trial or in the press.

Moreover, Dreiser's narrative reproduces some of the rhetorical strategies used by defense attorneys to argue against death sentences for their clients. Clyde's defense team, for example, considers the strategy used to save Harry Thaw from the electric chair: "Well, I'll tell you, Jephson, it's a tough case and no mistake. It looks to me now as though Mason has all the cards. If we can get this chap off, we can get anybody off. But as I see it, I'm not so sure that we want to mention that cataleptic business yet—at least not unless we want to enter a plea of insanity or emotional insanity, or something like that—about like that Harry Thaw case, for instance" (599).

Although Thaw is mentioned only briefly, Dreiser's audience would likely be more familiar with the case than with Gillette's. Within weeks of Gillette's murder of Billie Brown, Thaw, a wealthy socialite, shot and killed Stanford White in front of dozens of witnesses during a performance at a dinner theater atop Madison Square Garden. White was New York's most famous architect—his designs included the Washington Square arch and the building in which he was murdered—and also one of the city's most notorious womanizers. His design for Madison Square Garden included a private penthouse apartment that permitted him to pursue his extramarital interests.

Thaw, the son of a Pittsburgh man who had amassed a fortune in the coke market, had a history of bizarre and sometimes violent behavior. He had never worked and spent his allowance, reportedly more than eighty thousand dollars a year, on travel, parties, and prostitutes. When he married Evelyn Nesbit, a member of the famed Floradora Chorus burlesque show and former mistress of Stanford White, his father cut off his allowance, but his mother surreptitiously restored it.

On the night of the murders White was, uncharacteristically, dining alone. Thaw excused himself from the table where he was dining with Evelyn Nesbit Thaw, his wife, and another couple, walked to White's table, withdrew a handgun from his coat pocket, and fired three bullets into the architect's head. Thaw immediately surrendered, claiming that he had acted to avenge White's rape of Evelyn in the years before the Thaws married. He was eventually found not guilty "on the ground of his insanity at the time of the commission of the act" (jury's verdict quoted in Nash, 545). In delivering its decision, the jury endorsed the position, advanced by Thaw's attorneys, that Thaw suffered from *Dementia americana*, "a singularly American neurosis among males in the U.S. who believed that every man's wife was sacred" (Nash, 545).

Thaw's was arguably the most celebrated and publicized murder case the nation had yet produced. Interest did not end when Thaw was admitted to the New York State Asylum in 1906 for the Criminally Insane in Matteawan. He escaped from the asylum briefly in 1913 but was soon captured in Canada and returned. In 1915 he was declared sane and released. He took control of the family fortune, estimated at forty million dollars, and divorced his wife, who had conceived and given birth to a child during his institutionalization. In 1916 he was again arrested, this time for flying into a rage and horsewhipping a teenage boy named Fred Gump. The arrest led to another stint at Matteawan, but in 1922 Thaw was again declared sane and released. He spent the remaining twenty-five years of his life in an extended, well-publicized, and dissipated tour of European capitals.

Clyde Griffiths may bear little resemblance to Harry Thaw, but Dreiser's novel suggests that they shared a compulsion to murder.

Like the Harry Thaw depicted by Thaw's defense team, Clyde kills during a fit of temporary insanity or delirium. Just before the drowning, Clyde is in "a confused and turbulent state mentally, scarcely realizing the clarity or import of any particular thought or movement or act" (485). Throughout the scene Clyde seems dissociated from his own actions, and the journalistic, naturalistic tone that characterizes most of the narrative turns suddenly disjointed and expressionistic. Clyde hears disembodied voices urging him through the steps of his plan, and the repetitive call of a bird becomes a hallucinatory incantation. Later, awaiting execution, Clyde will recall that, during the death scene, "there had been a complex troubled state, bordering, as he now saw it, almost upon trance or palsy" (793).

Clyde's case is also like Thaw's in that both defendants are represented as enacting a peculiarly American pattern. Dreiser's account of the writing of his novel stresses that he saw Gillette's case as but one of many possible forms of American murder. That genre contained many variations on a basic plot:

> In the main, as I can show by the records, it was the murder of a young girl by an ambitious young man. . . . [One variation] was that of the young ambitious lover of some poorer girl, who in the earlier state of affairs had been attractive enough to satisfy him both in the matter of love and her social station. But nearly always with the passing of time and the growth of experience on the part of the youth, a more attractive girl with money or position appeared and he quickly discovered that he could no longer care for his first love. What produced this particular type of crime about which I am talking was the fact that it was not always possible to drop the first girl. What usually stood in the way was pregnancy, plus the genuine affection of the girl herself for her love, plus also her determination to hold him. [Quoted in Fishkin, 106]

Dreiser claimed familiarity with numerous cases fitting this pattern, and he settled on the Gillette case as his model only after starting two other novels based on similar murders. The parallels between the forms of temporary insanity that drive Clyde's and Thaw's actions heighten the contrast in the outcomes of the two trials.

The cumulative effect of Dreiser's rhetorical strategies is to call into question Clyde's responsibility for Roberta's death. If Clyde's actions follow a common pattern, then perhaps the ultimate source of those actions lies in his circumstance and not his inherent nature. If the judicial process that hands down Clyde's death sentence is a corrupt one, then the sentence itself may be unjust. If his actions spring from mental illness, then his responsibility for them is diminished. Beneath the apparent objectivity of Dreiser's novel there lies a kind of political allegory.

The two points of view represented by Norris and Dreiser may be regarded as sides in a debate over the causes of crime and the legitimacy of correctional authority. Norris naturalizes police power and the social hierarchy by equating them with biological law, while Dreiser depicts police power and class divisions as imposing unnatural restrictions on Clyde's natural instincts. Norris, like many biological determinists, envisions a continuum of power in which the police abet natural selection and evolutionary progress. Dreiser, siding with the environmental determinists, takes a less generous view; in *An American Tragedy*, crime is shown to be a product not of our animal past but of our human present.

In adapting Gillette's story, Dreiser saw his task as a corrective one. He perceived mistakes in the way the crime had been interpreted and reported, and he sought to correct those mistakes. He would later say that his study of the Gillette case convinced him "that there was an entire mis-understanding or perhaps I had better say misapprehension, of the conditions or circumstances surrounding the victims of that murder *before* the murder was committed" (quoted in Fishkin, 110). This misapprehension as depicted in the novel recalls the biological determinism of *McTeague* as well as the newspaper reports on the Patrick Collins case. Clyde is represented to the public as a "reptilian villain" (502) and a "murderer of the coldest and blackest type" (735).

While the prosecution labors to cast Clyde as a cold-blooded monster, the defense counters with a strategy more consonant with the events surrounding Roberta's death as the reader knows them: "Gentlemen of the jury, the individual on trial here for his life is a mental as well as a moral coward—no more and no less—not a downright, hardhearted criminal by any means. Not unlike many men in critical situations, he is a victim of a mental and moral fear complex" (669). The defense attorney's contention that Clyde is "not unlike many men in critical situations" signals one of the novel's central rhetorical strategies: the novel defends Clyde by blurring the distinction between the normal and the criminal.[2] This strategy places the novel squarely in conflict with the dominant discourse, which identifies a gap between normalcy and criminality. *McTeague*, in line with the dominant discourse of its time, portrays the capital murderer as an evolutionary throwback and radically different from normal humans.

An American Tragedy undermines the facile distinction between the normal and the criminal in a number of ways. The novel's corrective retelling of the Gillette case, for example, first alters some basic facts of that case that would make it more difficult to place Clyde within the spectrum of normalcy. The most significant change involves the manner of death. Gillette told several conflicting stories of Billie Brown's death and testified at his trial that she had leaped from the boat in order to commit suicide. The medical evidence demonstrated, however, that she had been violently and repeatedly struck about the head and shoulders while she drowned. In Clyde's case the medical evidence is much more ambiguous. Roberta's relatively minor injuries do not disprove Clyde's claim that the blow he struck was accidental. Dreiser's transformation of the alleged murder weapon likewise obscures Clyde's culpability. Gillette could offer no unincriminating explanation for taking a tennis racket along on the rowboat, but Clyde strikes Roberta with a camera. The camera, which could be used on a boat, is less damning as circumstantial evidence.

By introducing the possibility that Clyde struck Roberta accidentally, Dreiser changes the entire complexion of the case and eliminates many of the questions that typically dominate crime narrative. The reader knows who was in the boat with Roberta and what his motives were. The reader knows that Clyde struck Roberta and that Roberta was conscious when she went into the water. The reader even knows that although Clyde plotted cold-blooded murder, he found himself, momentarily at least, unable to carry out the plan. By reconstructing the Gillette case in this way, Dreiser shifts the reader's

---

[2]Shelley Fisher Fishkin, in "From Fact to Fiction: *An American Tragedy*," makes a similar claim, although in a somewhat different context, about the way Dreiser blurs the line between the normal and the criminal.

attention from the usual questions and toward diagnostic questions about state of mind. Whether or not Clyde struck the blow is less important than whether or not his actions were voluntary, involuntary, or accidental. The question of guilt is thus narrowed to the legal question of intent, of *mens rea*.

The novel does not answer the question directly. The blow, we are told, was "accidentally and all but unconsciously administered" (493). Even Clyde seems uncertain about Roberta's final moments. In prison, he "sat there, trying honestly now to think how it really was (exactly) and greatly troubled by his inability to demonstrate to himself even—either his guilt or his lack of guilt" (795). The confusion regarding Clyde's guilt may indicate Dreiser's belief that complex factors produce murder, and it certainly raises questions about the certainty with which judge and jury render their verdicts. There is simply no way for the court to prove or disprove Clyde's story.

The question of intent may also—appropriately—be considered in relation to Dreiser's well-documented interest in Freudian psychology. While writing *An American Tragedy*, Dreiser frequently discussed Freudian interpretations of murder and murderers with Dr. Abraham Brill, Freud's American translator. During this same period Brill completed and published his translation of Freud's *The Psychopathology of Everyday Life* (1924).

Freud's book purports to reveal the psychological underpinnings of everyday "accidents" and "absent-minded" behavior. Freud argues, of course, that there are no true accidents, and this idea provides us with perhaps the best context within which to consider Clyde's "accidental" killing of Roberta. Brill and Freud offer Dreiser a way to depict Clyde killing Roberta while simultaneously affirming his status as the puppet of deterministic forces. When Clyde strikes Roberta, he unconsciously carries out the plan concocted by his own poorly restrained id: "Indeed the center or mentating section of his brain at this time might well have been compared to a sealed and silent hall in which alone and undisturbed, and that in spite of himself, he now sat thinking on the mystic or evil and terrifying desires or advice of some darker or primordial and unregenerative nature of his own, and without the power to drive the same forth or himself to decamp, and yet also without the courage to act upon anything" (463). The novel

55

figures the id as malevolent genie to Clyde's Aladdin, and as "the very substance of some leering and diabolical wish or wisdom contained in [Clyde's] nature" (463–64).

The rewriting of Gillette's premeditated, brutal act of murder as ambiguous accident prepares us to understand Clyde as normal, and Dreiser's use of the Freudian paradigm furthers this purpose. Freud helps Dreiser establish that Clyde is extraordinary not because of his psychological structure but because of his circumstance. In fact, Clyde's motives and desires, when compared with those of the novel's other characters, prove quite ordinary. Like many Americans of humble origin, Clyde dreams of great wealth and high social station. Dreiser suggests that this cultural obsession with money and material success provides the true context in which we should understand cases like Gillette's. Dreiser would later comment that Clyde "was really doing the kind of thing which Americans should and would have said was the wise and moral thing to do . . . had he not committed a murder" (quoted in Fishkin, 110).

Having recast the most troublesome facts of the Gillette case so as to make it at least possible that Clyde struck Roberta accidentally, Dreiser was left with the still daunting task of portraying the plotter of cold-blooded murder as an ordinary boy victimized by circumstance. While the novelist was immersed in this task, the Chicago trial of Nathan Leopold and Richard Loeb for kidnapping and murder began receiving national attention. Clarence Darrow's eloquent defense of the two young men employs many of the rhetorical strategies that Dreiser uses to tell the story of Clyde Griffiths.

The story of Leopold and Loeb, like Clyde's, unfolds against a backdrop of money and privilege. The two teenagers, children of wealthy Chicago socialites, seemed destined for lives of luxury and success. At eighteen, Leopold, who had a prodigious intellect, became the youngest person to receive a B.Ph. from the University of Chicago. He was an avid student of philosophy, ornithology, and botany and spoke nine languages fluently. Leopold's friend Loeb was likewise a precocious student, the youngest ever to graduate from the University of Michigan at Ann Arbor. On May 20, 1924, apparently in an effort to prove themselves Nietzschean supermen, the two attempted to commit the perfect crime. Their plan required them to kidnap, murder, and then collect ransom for a child of a wealthy family in their neighborhood. They chose as their victim Bobbie Franks, who was fourteen years old and a distant cousin of Loeb's.

After murdering Franks and hiding his body, the two delivered the ransom note. The perfect plan of the boy geniuses, however, proved full of holes. Several different trails leading to Leopold and Loeb were discovered almost immediately, and the boys soon confessed. Leopold's father reportedly got down on his knees and promised Clarence Darrow one million dollars if he would take the case and save young Leopold from execution. Darrow, knowing that a jury would be inflamed by the sensational press coverage of the case, advised his clients to waive their right to a jury trial and plead guilty. In the month-long bench trial that followed, Darrow argued that his clients should be spared. He was successful. The judge sentenced each of the boys to life plus ninety-nine years.

Darrow's lengthy defense of his clients, and especially his widely reprinted closing remarks, may have been an important source for the defense of Clyde Griffiths. Richard Lingeman in his biography of Dreiser reports, "Dreiser had followed the Leopold-Loeb trial closely in 1924 while he was writing the *Tragedy*" (288). Lingeman contends that Dreiser "was more interested in the psychology of the murderers than in Darrow's tactics" (288), but the novelist's strategy clearly parallels Darrow's in a number of ways. Both emphasize environmental determinants of criminal behavior, and both plead for mercy on the basis of immaturity and mental disease. Just as Dreiser opposes the portrayal of his client as a reptilian monster, Darrow argues against claims, put forth by the prosecution and in the press, that his clients are cold-blooded "thrill-killers." He claims instead that his clients are relatively normal boys caught up in extraordinary circumstance.

Although the details of the two crimes differ, Darrow and Dreiser describe the social and economic contexts in similar terms. Both men, for example, depict accumulated wealth as a corrupting influence on everyone near it, particularly the young. When Darrow closes his defense of Leopold and Loeb, he blames wealth for their crimes: "We have grown to think that the misfortune is in not having [money]. The great misfortune in this terrible case is the money. That has de-

stroyed their lives. That has fostered these illusions. That has promoted this mad act" (*Attorney*, 63). Dreiser later echoed this interpretation of the link between wealth and crime in an essay written after
An American Tragedy had been published: "Yet even prosperity itself,
the prosperity that takes too much for the few and gives too little to
the many, foments outlawry. The madness of material things (most
of which are hideously inartistic, and yet in America encouraged by
every sort of price reduction and installment payment plan) makes
people run amuck, hooting and snorting to heap up more and more
possessions, mostly worthless, and lawfully or otherwise" ("Crime
and Why," in *Tragic America*, 299). In both examples, wealth and prosperity—which are fundamentally good in most versions of the American Dream—are linked to criminality.

In his mad quest for wealth, then, Clyde differs in degree but not
in kind from the American norm. In his desire for prosperity and
social advancement, he resembles most of the other characters in the
novel. When Hortense Briggs schemes to lure Clyde into buying her
a fur coat, and when the bellhops carouse at expensive restaurants
and brothels, they seek the trappings of wealth. By the same token,
the hope of a "newer and greater life" (245) causes Roberta to leave
her small hometown for the wider prospects and higher salaries available in Lycurgus. The same hope enters into her attraction to Clyde:
"Roberta, after encountering Clyde and sensing the superior world in
which she imagined he moved . . . was seized with the very virus of
ambition and unrest that afflicted him" (250). In all of these examples, the lure of prosperity seduces the young into some form of transgression. The gap between Clyde and his peers thus grows smaller.

Neither Darrow nor Dreiser, however, suggests that the desire for
prosperity corrupts only the young. Darrow accuses state attorneys of
sensationalizing the Leopold and Loeb case to inflate their reputa-
tions and further their careers (*Attorney*, 27). He also calls the testimony of Dr. Krohn, the state's psychological expert, "the cold, delib-
erate act of a man getting his living by dealing in blood" (39). Similar
considerations of money and social standing animate the individuals
involved in Clyde's prosecution and sentencing. As soon as the coroner sees Roberta's body, his thoughts turn to the upcoming elections.
He notes that such a case could benefit the incumbent district attor-

ney, "a close and helpful friend of his" (501). With a conviction in so infamous a case, the district attorney might carry his party's entire ticket—Coroner Heit included—to victory.

In the world of Dreiser's novel, even jurors are not free from such pragmatic considerations:

> And in the meantime the twelve men—farmers, clerks and storekeepers, re-canvassing for their own mental satisfaction the fine points made by Mason and Belknap and Jephson. Yet out of the whole twelve but one man—Samuel Upham, a druggist—(politically opposed to Mason and taken with the personality of Jephson)—sympathizing with Belknap and Jephson. And so pretending that he had doubts as to the completeness of Mason's proof until at last after five ballots were taken he was threatened with exposure and the public rage and obloquy which was sure to follow in case the jury were hung. "We'll fix you. You won't get by with this without the public knowing exactly where you stand." Whereupon, having a satisfactory drug business in North Mansfield, he at once decided that it was best to pocket this opposition to Mason and agree. [736–37]

Thus Dreiser, echoing Darrow, discredits the judicial process as an unbiased, clinically detached search for justice. He also resists the mainstream tendency to draw a hard and fast line between the normal and the criminal. The motives of the jurors, the attorneys, and the judge are strikingly similar to Clyde's motives, and in most matters Clyde embraces the values of his culture.

After indicting wealth and the pursuit of wealth as both the culprit in Bobbie Franks's murder and the motive behind the state's case for execution, Darrow's defense strategy focused on two factors that he considered mitigating. He said, "I think all of the facts of this extraordinary case, all of the testimony of the alienists, all that your honor has seen and heard, all their friends and acquaintances who have come to enlighten the court—I think all of it shows that this terrible act was the act of immature and diseased brains, the act of children" (79). Leopold and Loeb deserved mercy, Darrow argued, because of their age and because they were mentally ill. This same general approach informs Dreiser's treatment of Clyde's story.

The task of portraying Leopold and Loeb as children was not as straightforward as it might seem. One was eighteen and the other nineteen, and both were college graduates. Nevertheless, Darrow described his clients as "two minors, two children, who have no right to sign a note or make a deed" (*Attorney*, 25). He also suggested that the prosecutors, eager to mislead the court, had portrayed the boys as more mature than they really were: "Here is Dickie Loeb, and Nathan Leopold, and the State objects to anybody calling the one 'Dickie' and the other 'Babe' although everybody does, but they think they can hang them easier if their names are Richard and Nathan, so we will call them Richard and Nathan" (25).

Similar exchanges occur during Clyde's trial. The prosecutor argues that Clyde is "not a boy" but a "bearded man" and insists that his "mind is a mature, not an immature one" (642). The defense counters by charging the prosecution with deliberately misrepresenting Clyde's level of maturity: "The foolish and inexperienced, yet in every case innocent and unintentional, acts of a boy of fifteen or sixteen have been gone into before you gentlemen as though they were the deeds of a hardened criminal, and plainly with the intention of prejudicing you against this defendant, who . . . can be said to have lived as clean and energetic and blameless and innocent a life as any boy of his years anywhere. You have heard him called a man—a bearded man—a criminal and crime-soaked product of the darkest vomitings of hell. And yet he is but twenty-one" (665). The mitigating aspects of immaturity help explain why Clyde is a year younger than Chester Gillette at the time of the drowning and also, perhaps, why Roberta is five years older than Billie Brown.

Dreiser's narrator, although not as hyperbolic as Clyde's attorney, sides with the defense team when it pronounces adolescence a fundamental determinant of Clyde's character: "For to say the truth, Clyde had a soul that was not destined to grow up. He lacked decidedly that mental clarity and inner directing application that in so many permits them to sort out from the facts and avenues of life the particular thing or things that make for their direct advancement" (169). Even Darrow, who reviewed *An American Tragedy* for the *New York Evening Post Literary Review*, saw adolescence as the key to understanding Clyde's fate: "Without the slightest preparation, he faces puberty, with all its new emotions and luring calls" (reprinted in Salzman, 6).

The defenders of Clyde, Leopold, and Loeb, by portraying their clients as adolescents, hope to gain from judge and jury the sort of sympathetic understanding that adults reserve for children. In addition, however, they participate in a larger public debate over adolescence, and some elements of this debate seem to have left their mark upon Dreiser's novel. In the United States in the mid-1920s, adolescence stood at the center of the dispute between biological and environmental determinists. Both sides conceded that adolescence was commonly marked by turbulent and even criminal behavior, but they disagreed regarding the reason. The biological determinists and the eugenicists cited widespread reports of adolescent turbulence as proof that human personality and behavior acted out inherited scripts. Proponents of environmental determinism claimed that adolescent turbulence was guided by cultural forces and further hypothesized that members of some cultures would show no signs of adolescent turmoil.

During the very years that Dreiser spent writing *An American Tragedy*, Franz Boas, the nation's most prominent cultural determinist, was planning for a graduate student some research into the relative importance of hereditary and environmental factors in determining adolescent behavior. The student was Margaret Mead. The book describing her research and conclusions, *Coming of Age in Samoa* (1928), became one of the most widely read and influential texts in modern anthropology. In it, Mead argued that Samoan adolescents showed no signs of the turbulent, antisocial behavior common in their Western counterparts. The Samoan example, Mead argued, offered proof that cultural factors far outweigh hereditary ones in determining human personality and behavior.[3]

Mead's method—to compare the behavior of biologically similar subjects in very different environments—also forms the basis of Darrow's 1925 essay "The Edwardses and the Jukeses." Darrow's essay responds to Richard L. Dugdale's *"The Jukes": A Study in Crime, Pauperism, Disease, and Heredity* (1877). Dugdale, an inspector of jails for the state of New York, tells of his discovery that several members of the same extended family were simultaneously serving time, for various crimes, in a rural jail. Dugdale uses a genealogical history of the fam-

---

[3]It should be noted that Mead's assessment of Samoan culture has been challenged, most notably by Derek Freeman.

ily to demonstrate that crime is a form of biologically determined behavior prevalent in certain bloodlines. His essay is often cited in the writings of hereditarians and eugenicists, so much so that Darrow chooses it for public rebuttal.

The rebuttal compares two family histories: one beginning with Jonathan Edwards, the other with Max Jukes. The descendants of Edwards became college presidents, doctors, and clergymen, while those of Jukes became burglars, thieves, and prostitutes. Darrow counters the hereditarian analysis of the two histories, which emphasized inferior and superior bloodlines, by explaining the divergence in terms of political, economic, social, and geographical circumstance. In closing his defense of Leopold and Loeb, Darrow contended that adolescents were especially susceptible to just such circumstantial factors: "The whole life of childhood is a dream and an illusion, and whether they take one shape or another shape depends not upon the dreamy boy but on what surrounds him" (*Attorney*, 63).

Like both Darrow and Mead, Dreiser hews to the tenets of cultural determinism by comparing the lives of biologically similar individuals in vastly different surroundings. His novel documents a controlled experiment in which two boys of the same bloodline are raised in very different settings and meet with very different ends. The narrator often comments on the resemblance between Clyde and his cousin Gilbert, and the physical likeness heightens the contrast in their backgrounds. Clyde is born into near poverty. His ineffective parents afford him little education, and by the time adolescence strikes he is virtually alone in the world. He begins working in a somewhat disreputable environment at an early age and begins living as a solitary fugitive in his midteens. Without the safety net provided by a strong family or by a secure position in a stable social group, Clyde is defenseless against adolescence and its accompanying turbulence. Gilbert's parents, in contrast, provide him with a secure and ordered home life, an expensive education, and a well-salaried position in the family business. He is guided through adolescence by stern, loving parents and protected from its pitfalls by social and financial buffers. Had Clyde taken Gilbert's place, Dreiser seems to tell us, he would have turned out as well or better.

The stress of Clyde's adolescence nicely accommodates the argument that he is relatively normal. It also helps resolve an apparent contradiction in Dreiser's defense strategy. The effort to depict Clyde as normal conflicts with the view that he suffered from temporary insanity. How can Clyde be both normal and insane? The answer, as Darrow notes, is that adolescence and insanity are linked: "Both these boys are in the adolescent age. Both these boys, as every alienist in this case on both sides tells you, are in the most trying period in the life of a child—both these boys, when the call of sex is new and strange; both these boys, at a time of seeking to adjust their young lives to the world, moved by the strongest feelings and passions that ever moved men; both these boys, at the time boys grow insane, at the time crimes are committed" (*Attorney*, 65). The volatile nature of adolescence in our society, then, helps Dreiser locate the source of Clyde's insanity in his circumstances rather than in his identity. If Clyde's motives and desires resemble those of many of his peers, his extraordinary situation most certainly does not, and adolescence makes Clyde all the more susceptible to its stress.

Clyde's situation is extraordinary because, unlike most of his working-class peers, he has a chance to move rapidly up the social scale. Like the other killers of whom Dreiser speaks, Clyde is caught between social classes. His blood tie to the Griffithses of Lycurgus gives him temporary access to high society, and marriage to Sondra Finchley would bring wealth enough to make this access permanent. The promise of prosperity, however, is attended by a tremendous amount of stress, stress perhaps best understood in terms of Dreiser's reading of Freud.

Clyde's sex drive may be typical for an adolescent, but as his social prospects widen, his opportunities for sexual release are proportionally restricted. When Clyde is promoted to foreman in his uncle's factory, Gilbert warns him that his new position is precarious and makes it clear that the chief obstacle to Clyde's success is a sexual one:

"This plant is practically operated by women from cellar to roof. In the manufacturing department, I venture to say that here are ten women to every man. On that account everyone in whom we entrust any responsibility around here must be known to us as to their moral and religious character. If you weren't related to us, and if we didn't feel that because of that we knew a little something about you, we wouldn't think of putting

63

you up there or anywhere in this factory over anybody until we did know. But don't think that because you're related to us that we won't hold you strictly to account for everything that goes on up there and for your conduct. We will, and all the more so because you are related to us." [232]

Gilbert ends by admonishing Clyde: "Not the least little thing must occur in connection with you that any one can comment on unfavorably" (233).

Clyde's precarious position between social classes thus places him under such relentless scrutiny that he is cut off from sexual release far more completely than his unmarried peers in either the upper classes or the lower. This atmosphere of surveillance is most apparent in the scenes depicting Clyde working at the head of the stamping department. Clyde is intensely aware of the women in the room and entertains sexual fantasies about several of them. Yet he is always aware that his every move is being watched. The feeling is not mere paranoia; every woman in the department studies Clyde for signs of sexual interest in one or another of the workers. Also, because he bears the Griffiths name and resembles his cousin Gilbert, Clyde finds this atmosphere of surveillance extended to every aspect of his life in Lycurgus. Initially, Clyde resolves to meet the challenge: "So elated was he at the moment that he bustled out of the great plant with a jaunty stride, resolved among other things that from now on, come what might, and as a test of himself in regard to life and work, he was going to be all that his uncle and cousin obviously expected of him—cool, cold even, and if necessary severe, where these women or girls of this department were concerned. No more relations with Dillard or Rita or anybody like that for the present anyhow" (234). Clyde later pursues an affair with Roberta but only in secrecy and only while his prospects for social advancement seem dim. He ends the affair when he realizes that he might actually be able to marry Sondra.

Clyde's predicament separates him from his counterparts, whose social status is unlikely to change. If Clyde were a factory worker with no hope of social advancement, any sexual indiscretion would go virtually unnoticed. The novel's descriptions of the other workers make it clear that they engage in sexual activity without significant risk to their social positions or jobs. As a career factory worker, Clyde might visit a brothel, just as he does while working as a bellhop. He would also have little reason to avoid marrying Roberta and easier access to birth control and abortion: "If only he could get her out of this! If only he could. But how, without money, intimates, a more familiar understanding of the medical or if not that exactly, then the sub rosa world of sexual freemasonry which some at times—the bell-hops of the Green-Davidson, for instance, seemed to understand" (408). If, on the other hand, Clyde were born to wealth, if he were Gilbert's brother and not his cousin, then he would likewise be allowed some form of sexual release. He could, presumably, visit a brothel, or perhaps "trifle" with some young woman from the lower classes, and he could do so without risking banishment.

When sons of the novel's wealthy do get in trouble with daughters of the underclass, there are ways to rectify the situation without severing family ties. Alvin Belknap, one of Clyde's attorneys and the son of a prominent politician, was once extricated from a situation much like Clyde's:

> In his twentieth year, he himself had been trapped between two girls, with one of whom he was merely playing while being seriously in love with the other. And having seduced the first and being confronted with an engagement or flight, he had chosen flight. But not before laying the matter before his father, by whom he was advised to take a vacation, during which time the services of the family doctor were engaged with the result that for a thousand dollars and expenses necessary to house the pregnant girl in Utica, the father had finally extricated his son and made possible his return, and eventual marriage to the other girl. [592–93]

For most members of society, Dreiser seems to be telling us, the social structure permits the controlled release of sexual tension and also provides remedies when "problems" arise. But for those few members of the underclass who are offered the possibility of rapid, effortless elevation to the aristocracy—the common ingredient in Dreiser's American genre of murder—intense scrutiny and precarious social standing combine to prohibit sexual activity, with the result that libidinal pressure builds to intolerable levels.

Unlike Belknap, Clyde cannot expect anyone to solve the problem of Roberta's pregnancy for him. His ties to the Lycurgus Griffithses are so weak that he finds himself living on a kind of probation. The family might rescue Gilbert from such a situation, but Clyde, a nephew and a virtual stranger, would likely be abandoned. This same probationary status prevents Clyde from finding help among the working class. As a Griffiths living in Lycurgus, Clyde is so widely recognized and so visible that by revealing his predicament to anyone he would risk gossip and exposure. Clyde's pathology, then, is not in his soul but in his situation.

The extraordinary pressures brought to bear on Clyde produce a mental illness much like the one said to have driven Leopold and Loeb. The two were portrayed in the press and by the prosecution as intellectual giants, and Darrow was able to turn this characterization to his advantage. He does so by demonstrating, at great length, that the plan concocted by the two supposed geniuses was dangerously ill conceived and destined to fail:

> The State says, in order to make out the wonderful mental processes of these two boys, that they fixed up a plan to go to Ann Arbor to get a typewriter, and yet when they got ready to do this act, they went down the street a few doors from their house and bought a rope; they went around the corner and bought acid; they went somewhere else nearby and bought tape; they went down to the hotel and rented a room, and then gave it up, and went to another hotel, and rented one there. And then Dick Loeb went to the hotel room, took a valise containing his library card and some books from the library, left it two days in the room, until the hotel took the valise and took the books. Then he went to another hotel and rented another room. He might just as well have sent his card with the ransom letter. [Darrow, *Attorney,* 33]

Premeditation, which should serve the interests of the prosecution, is thus transformed into a mitigating factor: "But we are told that they planned. Well, what does that mean? A maniac plans, an idiot plans, an animal plans, any brain that functions may plan; but their plans were the diseased plans of the diseased mind" (Darrow, *Attorney,* 41).

Clyde's plan to murder Roberta proves to be similarly flawed. Despite his elaborate attempts at secrecy, authorities discover Clyde's identity almost immediately. As soon as Roberta's body is found, incriminating evidence begins to surface. A man matching the description of the drowned woman's companion is seen later that night walking furtively through the woods, dressed in a suit and carrying a suitcase. The bruises on Roberta's face suggest violence. An examination of the items Roberta left at the inn reveals further reason for alarm. Clyde and Roberta do not register under their true names, but in Roberta's coat investigators find a letter addressed to her mother detailing her plans to marry. A subsequent conversation with Roberta's mother leads the authorities directly to Clyde. Even if Roberta had not told her mother Clyde's name, the local postman could have provided it; he remembers that Roberta had mailed as many as fifteen letters to Clyde Griffiths in Lycurgus during the weeks preceding her death. When the letters are found in Clyde's room—along with letters from Sondra—they provide a narrative account of his motive for murder. In Roberta's suitcase, left at the inn, authorities find a toilet set with a card that reads "For Bert from Clyde—Merry Xmas" (519).

The incriminating clues accumulate so quickly and in such number that the district attorney wonders, at least momentarily, whether Clyde is innocent. "Would a man contemplating murder fail to see a card such as this, with his own handwriting on it? What sort of plotter and killer would that be?" (520). Dreiser, perhaps following Darrow's lead, suggests that Clyde's plan fails miserably because it was conceived during a fit of temporary insanity. "There are moments when in connection with the sensitively imaginative or morbidly anachronistic—the mentality assailed and the same not of any great strength and the problem confronting it of sufficient force and complexity—the reason not actually toppling from its throne, still totters or is warped or shaken—the mind befuddled to the extent that for the time being at least, unreason or disorder and mistaken or erroneous counsel would appear to hold against all else" (463). Dreiser characterizes Clyde not as insane but as normal, a young man temporarily unbalanced by environmental stress. Mental disease deprives Clyde, like Leopold and Loeb, of the ability to reason—both intellectually and morally. Like Harry Thaw, Clyde comes temporarily under the spell of an irresistible impulse whose shape bears the peculiar, even unique, stamp of American culture.

In *An American Tragedy*, Dreiser dismantles the diagnostic biography of an executable offender with remarkable thoroughness. Gillette is portrayed in the press as a cold-blooded killer, but Clyde is a mentally ill coward who may even be innocent of the crime for which he is executed. In the press accounts, Gillette, like McTeague, is described as biologically programmed to murder; Clyde, however, is a victim and the product of circumstance. The state argues that Clyde is fundamentally criminal, a moral imbecile or reptile. The novel shows that his character was determined by the values of his society. Had Clyde been born into a more hospitable environment, his life need not have ended in the electric chair. Had society not teased him with wealth and power while simultaneously condemning him to mindless labor and low pay, he need not have killed. Had the officials charged with evaluating Clyde's life and crime not been blinded by their own greed, they would not have delivered a sentence of death.

It is clear, then, that the novel declares its opposition to the dominant carceral discourse, but assessing the effectiveness of such opposition is a complex task. Careful examination may reveal that Dreiser's narrative is built on assumptions about criminality and normalcy that, while overtly opposed to the dominant carceral discourse, nevertheless serve the interests of carceral power.

In *Discipline and Punish*, Foucault makes the arresting observation that the modern criminal justice system has been attacked, virtually from its inception, in ways that paradoxically call for strengthening and extending the power to imprison. Again and again, in a pattern that persists to this day, critics have complained that prison does nothing to reduce crime and in fact encourages delinquency. And yet the "answer to these criticisms was invariably the same: the reintroduction of the invariable principles of penitentiary technique. For a century and a half the prison had always been offered as its own remedy: the reactivation of the penitentiary techniques as the only means of overcoming their perpetual failure; the realization of the corrective project as the only way of overcoming the impossibility of implementing it" (268). By identifying failures in the criminal justice system, critics may call, directly or indirectly, for the very reforms that ensure its continued operation and expansion.

Dreiser's novel can likewise be seen to criticize certain elements of our criminal justice system in ways that potentially serve the interests of the power it embodies. The tragedy of Clyde's case, for example, results from a diagnostic failure. Clyde is deliberately misdiagnosed so that attorneys, judges, and jurors can further their careers. He differs greatly in personality and type from the other inmates of Death Row.

The other condemned men are described in language that recalls both the racism that underlies much biological determinism and the sensationalized coverage of crime in the popular press. The first inmate whom Clyde notices is "a sallow and emaciated and sinister-looking Chinaman in a suit exactly like his own, who had come to the bars of his door and was looking at him out of inscrutable slant eyes" (755). Other inmates are described in similar terms:

> The two dark-eyed and sinister-looking Italians, one of whom had slain a girl because she would not marry him; the other who had robbed and then slain and attempted to burn the body of his father-in-law in order to get money for his wife! And big Larry Donahue—square-headed, square-shouldered—big of feet and hands, an overseas soldier, who, being ejected from a job as night watchman in a Brooklyn factory, had lain for the foreman who had discharged him—and then killed him in an open common somewhwere at night, but without the skill to keep from losing a service medal, which had eventually served to betray and identify him. . . . And Thomas Mowrer . . . a man who had killed his employer with a pitchfork . . . a rude, strong, loutish man of about thirty, who looked more beaten and betrayed than as though he had been able to torture or destroy another. [768]

Clyde's case is tragic because he is improperly diagnosed and placed on Death Row with born murderers. The novel attacks not so much capital punishment, then, as the mistakes made in administering it. The misdiagnosis of Clyde on which his execution rests in no way fundamentally challenges the idea that executable murderers can be distinguished from nonexecutable murderers through a scientifically informed diagnosis. Instead, the narrative seems to reaffirm the importance of the diagnostic task. If people so very different from one another can be convicted under the same statute, then the only hope for appropriate sentencing is a more painstaking and more accurate diagnostic procedure. Only through heightened vigilance and increased attention to diagnosis can tragedies like Clyde's execution be avoided.

Attempts to distinguish dominant from resistant discourse are further complicated by the fact that the social significance of the discourse surrounding capital punishment is not limited to the task of diagnosing executable offenders. Only a tiny fraction of the felons eligible for the death sentence actually receive it, but the diagnostic narratives used in selecting the condemned have wide-ranging implications. Diagnostic biographies naturalize various categories of criminal—including the executable offender—but as we have seen, they also naturalize the normal, law-abiding citizen. By defining both the normal and the criminal, these narratives legitimize regulatory powers that extend far beyond prison walls. Furthermore, because the two functions may operate independently—the one focused on the individual offender, the other broadcast toward the general population—texts that openly disagree on a particular diagnosis may nonetheless share assumptions about criminality and normalcy.

In sum, narrative can overtly declare its opposition to the dominant discourse and nevertheless support the penal project. In addition, the diagnostic biography used to identify the executable offender can also serve to police the normal. Critical evaluations of the execution novel might accommodate these facts by focusing on the way in which a novel manipulates the images of danger associated with crime. Execution novels, like the diagnostic biographies from which they derive, trace brutal crimes to their antecedents in a broad range of "abnormal" behaviors and characteristics. These behaviors and characteristics may themselves be legal and even harmless, but when linked to capital crimes they acquire an aura of danger.

An American Tragedy uses the rhetoric of danger to promote normalization partly in its treatment of sexuality. When Clyde carouses with the other bellhops from the Green-Davidson, and especially when he accompanies them to a house of prostitution, he takes the first in a series of steps that will lead him to the death house. Later, when he seduces Roberta, the encounter is marked by an almost palpable sense of impending doom: "And Clyde feeling, and not unlike Roberta, who was firmly and even painfully convinced of it, that this was sin—deadly, mortal—since both his mother and father had so often emphasized that—the seducer—adulterer—who preys outside the sacred precincts of marriage. And Roberta, peering nervously into the blank future, wondering what—how, in any case, by any chance, Clyde should change, or fail her" (299). Clyde's plan to kill Roberta stems directly from an illicit affair that significantly offends both Christian decency and his company's policy. The link between illicit sexuality and crime, professional failure, and danger is also evident in the novel's suggestion that people who lead successful lives avoid sexual impropriety. When Clyde begins working as a bellhop at the prestigious Union League Club of Chicago, he is struck by the fact that the men who frequent the club (no women are allowed) betray no interest in sexual matters. Clyde concludes that "one could not attain or retain one's place in so remarkable a world as this unless one were indifferent to sex" (169).

Illicit sexuality is only one source of danger identified in the novel. The danger represented by people like Clyde is also linked to failures within the family and departures from traditional family values. Clyde's weak, vacillating character is largely a product of his early family life, and the novel seems to single out Asa, his father, for special blame: "To begin with, Asa Griffiths, the father, was one of those poorly integrated and correlated organisms, the product of an environment and a religious theory, but with no guiding or mental insight of his own, yet sensitive and therefore highly emotional and without any practical sense whatsoever" (13). Asa's inability to provide a stable, financially secure environment for his family causes Clyde to develop in two ways that will eventually lead him to plot murder. From a very early age, Clyde becomes "conscious of the fact that the work his parents did was not satisfactory to others,—shabby, trivial," and he dreams of bettering himself. These dreams take no practical form, however, because Clyde's parents "did not understand the . . . necessity for some of practical or professional training for each and every one of their young ones" (14). Lacking a practical education, Clyde attempts to achieve his dreams of wealth through marriage and through murder.

Had Clyde been raised in a more "normal" family, he might not have yielded so easily to the temptations of murder and illicit sex. The normal counterpart to Clyde's abnormal family is embodied by the Lycurgus Griffithses, a branch of the family headed by a man characterized as Asa's exact opposite. When Clyde first meets Samuel

71

Griffiths, he notes that "his uncle appeared to be so quick, alert, incisive—so very different from his father in every way" (171). Samuel Griffiths is a shrewd businessman and a stern, effective father. As a result his children grow into law-abiding citizens. By suggesting that weak fathers like Asa can produce children capable of capital murder, the novel polices family life. Individual failures to live up to the ideals of middle-class morality and Christian decency are exposed as dangers to the entire society.

The novel's treatment of adolescence complements this tendency to link familial abnormality to crime and dangerous behavior. Dreiser's narrative criminalizes adolescence by portraying it as the time in our lives when we are most apt to give in to criminal urges and temptations. The novel thus suggests that both society and the family have the responsibility of policing and disciplining adolescents. Clyde needed, and did not get, the stern tutelage of a strong father. He should never have been exposed to the easy money and seedy life enjoyed by bellhops working in luxury hotels. Roberta should never have been allowed to leave her parents' farm for factory work in another town, nor should she have been allowed to rent a room in a bad part of town, away from the watchful eyes of older friends and relatives. The inherently turbulent and even criminal nature of puberty in American society demands that adolescents be held under strict supervision.

In identifying the antecedents of dangerous criminality, however, the novel designates extramarital sex, abnormal family life, inadequate education, and adolescence as significant but secondary. The primary focus is on the American dream of success and social advancement. Because the doors to America's aristocracy are not entirely closed, and because all American schoolchildren are taught that wealth and luxury are both desirable and generally available, people like Clyde will be placed in stressful situations that they would not have to endure in societies with more clearly defined social boundaries. The American dream may provide a blueprint for success for a tiny fraction of the nation's youth, but accepting that dream also means that a normal working life, the life that the vast majority of Americans must lead, is tragically devalued. For Clyde, working-class

existence is so onerous that he will attempt anything—even murder—to escape it.

The novel's critique of the American dream seems intended to miti-
gate Clyde's responsibility for Roberta's death. Clyde plots murder
not because he is inherently evil but because he is born into poverty,
raised by incompetent parents, and forced to make his way alone
during adolescence. Dreiser may have been calling for a more humane approach to crime, but the underlying assumption is nevertheless that the uneducated poor are the most dangerous members of
society. Darrow, whose arguments about the nature of crime provided
an important source for Dreiser, treats the underclass with a similarly
paradoxical mix of fear and sympathy:

> What we call civilization has moved so fast that the structure and instincts
> of man have not been able to become adjusted to it. The structure is too
> cumbersome, too intense, too hard, and if not breaking down of its own
> weight, it is at least destroying thousands who cannot adjust themselves
> to its changing demands. Not only are the effects of this growing body of
> social and legal restrictions shown by their constant violation, generally by
> the inferior and the poor, but indirectly in their strain on the nervous
> system; by the irritation and impatience they generate, and which, under
> certain conditions cause acts of violence. [*Crime*, 43]

Clyde cannot withstand the strain of his situation because his background and his childhood experience leave him with no stable identity. He remakes himself to match each new environment and thus
lacks the moral fortitude to resist temptation. Even as the novel
shows why Clyde should not be blamed for his actions, it demonstrates that he is hopelessly dangerous.

Dreiser traces the danger associated with capital crime back to its
various sources. In so doing, he advertises his novel as a humane
countermyth that corrects fatal errors in the diagnostic biography of
the executable offender. As *An American Tragedy* works to discredit
the fundamental assumption of diagnostic biography, however—that
some people are inherently and immutably criminal—it naturalizes a
new, situational model of the dangerous individual. The source of
Clyde's crime may lie outside his body, but it lies within aspects of the
social structure that are absolutely fundamental to American culture.

Dreiser's narrative suggests that when the poor are allowed access to affluent communities, they may be possessed by irresistible criminal urges. As long as some Americans are rich and others are poor, as long as the borders between social classes remain semipermeable, some number of people in Clyde's situation will be driven to act as he does. Social contact between the poor and the affluent, then, is the novel's most dangerous circumstance.

An American Tragedy illustrates just how easily a dissenting text can be made to serve the interests of the opposing viewpoint. As demonstrated above, the novel interprets crime in a way that encourages people of low social status to engage in "normal" behavior: they should avoid extramarital sex, learn a trade, adhere to company policy, maintain traditional families, and vigorously discipline their adolescent children. Otherwise social advancement may escape them. By supporting a "scientific" criminology that naturalizes criminal activity in poor populations, the novel also discourages social contact between rich and poor and justifies the residential and social segregation of social classes. The novel's comingling of dissent and complicity suggests that overtly resistant discourse must be evaluated on the basis of what it does, not what it claims to do.

If it had not been for these thing . . . , I might have live out
my life talking at street corners to scorning men. I might have
die, unmarked, unknown, a failure. Now we are not a failure.
This is our career and our triumph. Never in our full life could
we hope to do such work for tolerance, for joostice, for man's
onderstanding of man as now we do by accident.

—Last speech to court by Bartolomeo Vanzetti

If, nevertheless, the author of a book of this sort is expected
to hazard a guess publicly, I may say that the only differences
I expect to see revealed between the behavior of rat and man
(aside from enormous differences of complexity) lie in the
field of verbal behavior.

—B. F. Skinner, *The Behavior of Organisms*

FOUR

Richard Wright's *Native Son:*
Rhetorical Determinism

Native Son, like *An American Tragedy*, is a protest novel, an extended
defense of a murderer that was intended to rebut the state's plea for
death. Like Dreiser, Wright notes that the killer would be spared if he
were wealthy and that in a more equitable society he might not have
been driven to kill. Although Wright's argument opposes the state's,
both sides seek the meaning of the offender's crimes in the story of
his life. Alone in his jail cell, awaiting trial, Bigger "knew as he stood
there that he could never tell why he had killed. It was not that he
did not really want to tell, but the telling of it would have involved
the telling of his entire life" (356).

Native Son may not tell Bigger's entire life story, but it narrates and
interprets more than he himself ever could. It brings to his biography

the sweep and depth of the naturalist novel. Wright apparently modeled his book quite consciously on *An American Tragedy*. Speaking to Margaret Walker, he defended his use of newspaper accounts of a celebrated Chicago murder trial with reference to Dreiser's adaptation of the Gillette case. Like Dreiser, too, Wright turned for inspiration to Chicago's most notorious murder. When he visited Chicago to research the novel, he went to a public library and "checked out two books on the Loeb-Leopold case and on Clarence Darrow" (Walker, 123–25).

The influence of Dreiser's novel and Darrow's defense of Leopold and Loeb on *Native Son*, however, is not readily apparent in the details and twists of plot. The novel tells the story of Bigger Thomas, who is first seen at age nineteen, living in a "Black Belt" Chicago ghetto, in a one-room kitchenette apartment he shares with his mother, sister, and brother. The story opens as the family rises on the day of Bigger's interview for a job as a chauffeur with a prominent and wealthy white family. Within hours of his hiring, Bigger is told to drive Mary Dalton, the daughter of his new employer, to an evening class at the local university. Mary is actually on her way to meet Jan Erlone, her Communist boyfriend. The two force Bigger to accompany them on their secret date and even to dine with them in a restaurant. Later, as Bigger returns Mary to the Dalton house, he finds that she is too drunk to walk, and he helps her to her bedroom. The moment is ripe with sexual tension. Just when it appears that some sort of romantic encounter will take place, Mary's blind mother enters the room. In an attempt to keep Mary quiet so that his presence in the room will not be discovered, Bigger covers her face with a pillow, suffocating her.

After realizing what he has done, and concluding that no one will believe his explanation, Bigger decides to dispose of the body and shift the blame to Jan and his comrades. He burns the corpse in the coal furnace after decapitating it to make it fit. He even concocts a plan to extort a ransom payment from the Daltons while further incriminating local Communists. The authorities initially overlook Bigger as a suspect and believe that Mary has run away or has been kidnapped, but when her remains are discovered, Bigger flees and goes into hiding. While he is a fugitive, Bigger murders Bessie, his

girlfriend, in cold blood. Soon afterward he is captured. After a per-
functory courtroom battle over execution, he is sentenced to death.
The novel ends moments before the sentence is to be carried out.

The opposition between environmental and biological determinism
informs *Native Son* as it does *An American Tragedy* and *McTeague*. The
novel tells the life story that Bigger cannot articulate. It depicts Bigger
not as a born murderer but as a man made murderous by his society's
ability to define him as such and by the harsh conditions under which
he has lived. Although the Chicago newspapers describe Bigger as a
"jungle beast" whose muscular arms hang "in a dangling fashion
to his knees" (322–23), the novel as a whole undermines biological
explanations of Bigger's behavior. Again and again Wright reminds
readers of the ways in which environmental forces shape his personality and also of the ease with which his life story may be erased and
rewritten as ideological parable. Wright's work also highlights the
role played by race in capital punishment, an aspect of the debate
that the two earlier novels did not address. *Native Son* informs its
readers that discussions of biological determinism in the United
States, at least where human behavior is concerned, are always about
race.

The deterministic forces that produce Bigger resemble those that
produced Clyde Griffiths, but Wright's novel makes them seem even
more powerful by emphasizing the role played by public discourse,
rather than chance, in creating them. Clyde's crime may have been
caused by an unjust social structure, but it also lay at the end of a
string of unlikely coincidences. The grim logic of Bigger Thomas's
world leaves less to chance. From the moment he enters the Dalton
house until the moment Mary is dead, Bigger is not allowed to choose
or decide anything. Moreover, he is branded a rapist and murderer at
a time when he is neither. A rough draft of his diagnostic biography
appears in the press. When Bigger eventually does rape and murder,
he seems almost to be surrendering to society's definition of him.
Despite the fact that he does not intentionally murder Mary, he concludes that "it seems sort of natural-like, me being here facing that
death chair. Now I come to think of it, it seems like something like
this just had to be" (415).

The influence of Dreiser and Darrow on *Native Son* is most evident, then, not in the mechanics of plot, but in the politics of interpretation and in the courtroom tactics of Boris Max, Bigger's attorney. When Max decides to have Bigger plead guilty and to concentrate on avoiding the death penalty, he replicates Darrow's defense strategy for Leopold and Loeb. The prosecutors who complain that the defense cannot "plead that boy both guilty and insane," voice the same objection that was raised by prosecutors facing Darrow (430). Like Darrow, Max argues that Bigger's behavior was determined by forces outside of his control and that he is thus not fully responsible for his crimes. Max tells the court, "In our blindness we have so contrived and ordered the lives of men that the moths in their hearts flutter toward ghoulish and incomprehensible flames!" (467).

Max's lengthy speeches are an attempt to historicize the killings, to depict them as natural consequences of slavery, of racial oppression through segregation, of Jim Crow law and lynch law. Max asks that we understand Bigger's crimes not as the actions of an individual but as the inevitable products of a particular social structure. Bigger's trial thus represents "not injustice, but *oppression*, an attempt to throttle or stamp out a new form of life. And it is this new form of life that has grown up in our midst that puzzles us, that expresses itself, like a weed growing from under a stone, in terms we call crime" (455).

Like Darrow, Max also suggests that the public's desire for the death penalty reflects a dangerous, shortsighted lust for blood: "The surest way to make sure that there will be more such murders is to kill this boy. In your rage and guilt, make thousands of other black men and women feel that the barriers are tighter and higher! Kill him and swell the tide of pent-up lava that will some day break loose, not in a single, blundering, accidental, individual crime, but in a wild cataract of emotion that will brook no control" (455–56).

Darrow's defense of Leopold and Loeb may offer Wright a source for Max's defense of Bigger, but Bigger's is a far different case. Leopold and Loeb, after all, escaped the death penalty, and they were wealthy and white. Bessie inspires Bigger to write the ransom note when she reminds him that she worked for neighbors of the Loebs at the time of Bobbie Franks's murder, but the reference is likely to suggest to Wright's readers not that the cases are parallel but that the contrast between them is ironic. In Bigger's world, as in that of Leopold and Loeb, the rich do not hang, and racial tension threatens to erase the line between the criminal justice system and the lynch mob.

Before the publication of *Native Son*, Richard Wright was a relatively obscure author. *Uncle Tom's Children*, a collection of stories published two years earlier, had been well received but in no way anticipated the success of *Native Son*. The commercial aspect of this success came about when the Book of the Month Club made the novel its main selection for March of 1940. In its first three weeks, *Native Son* sold 215,000 copies. In 1941, the year that *Citizen Kane* was released, Orson Welles directed a stage adaptation of the novel. Within a few years, Wright had risen from anonymity to national and international renown and had come to be regarded as one of the most successful and talented writers of his generation.

Merely by choosing racial tension as his topic, however, Wright aroused controversy prior to publication that obliged him to change the text. The Book of the Month Club predicated its selection of *Native Son* on Wright's willingness to make certain alterations.[1] He was asked to make the encounter between Bigger and Mary in her room less overtly sexual and to remove or at least tone down a scene in which Bigger and Jack masturbated in the movie theater. Wright complied with these requests, but at the same time he removed evidence of the scene that immediately followed the masturbation scene. In the original version, Jack and Bigger see a titillating newsreel in which the daughters of the nation's rich are shown vacationing in Florida. The story features footage of Mary Dalton and Jan Erlone cavorting on the beach and includes a report that Mary's family ended her vacation early and called her home and away from the young radical. Bigger, who recognizes Mary as the daughter of his prospective employer, immediately begins speculating about the opportunities that may accompany his new position.

Why would Wright want to exclude this scene (and the half dozen or so references to it later in the novel)? Thematically, the scene is

---

[1] The original manuscript of *Native Son*, as approved by Wright, was published in 1991 by the Library of America in a series entitled *Early Works*. Unless otherwise noted, page citations for quoted material refer to this restored version.

important because it shows that when Bigger is employed by the Daltons, he enters the world of glamour and fantasy that he has previously known only through films and magazines. Less than twelve hours after Bigger sees Mary on the silver screen, he will take her on an illicit date with Jan, eat and drink at her table, and watch her engage in a drunken, amorous interlude in the car's back seat. Later, finding himself alone with her in her bedroom in the middle of the night, he will kiss her and fondle her breasts. By the next day his friends will all be saying that Bigger sat in a restaurant, eating and drinking beer with people whose lives are chronicled in newsreels.

Perhaps the best way to explain the removal from the novel of the newsreel featuring Jan and Mary is to look at what Wright puts in its place. In the revised version, the showing of *Trader's Horn* becomes a double feature with the addition of *The Gay Woman*. Both films seem to comment on the action of the novel, and taken together they provide a kind of shorthand statement of important themes. *Trader's Horn* tells the story of Europeans in colonial Africa. The central plot, involving white characters, is played out against a backdrop of "naked black men and women whirling in wild dances" (36). *The Gay Woman* tells an improbable tale of adultery among the ultrarich, a tale in which a narrowly thwarted assassination attempt by a wild-eyed, bomb-throwing Communist prompts two lovers to repent and end their affair. The substitution of *The Gay Woman* for the newsreel makes little sense as part of a publisher's attempt to tone down racy or otherwise offensive content, but it does allow Wright to widen greatly the scope of the novel's commentary on public discourse and power. When readers discover that Bigger sees Mary and Jan on the screen on the same day he meets them, the unlikely coincidence is enough to overshadow anything the scene might say about the relationship between crime and popular narrative. By replacing the newsreel with the feature films, Wright eliminates the distracting coincidence. He draws our attention away from a particular newsreel about Bigger's new employers and directs it instead toward whole genres of popular narratives about white and black, rich and poor, savage and civilized.

These narratives exercise power by dehumanizing people, individually or in groups, thus justifying their treatment as less than human. Such narratives can also manipulate images of danger, to encourage

80

people to avoid certain behaviors and situations. The romanticization of outlaw heroes can lure hopeless young men into a life of violent crime. Wright, like Dreiser, suggests that U.S. society incites some people to murderous violence by bombarding them with images of wealth and glamour, images that teach them to want a life that they cannot have and to devalue the life they do have. The stories that convey these images, including the biography that society has prepared for Bigger, should therefore be read not for their overt meaning but as allegories of political domination and resistance. In *Native Son*, Wright demonstrates that the fate of the individual lies in the hands of the biographer and that stories express the society that created them.

Wright gained his reputation as a man of letters and a social commentator in the years following the publication of *Native Son*. The initial flurry of publicity, however, presented him not as a social critic but as a juvenile delinquent who had saved himself from a life of crime through a determined and willful act of self-education. The brief article on Wright that appeared in the *New York Sun* in the spring of 1940 described him as someone who had once seemed destined for the penitentiary or even Death Row: "Richard Wright is a Negro who has had slightly more than eight years of schooling, who was a bad boy, who has been on relief, on WPA, a street cleaner and a ditch-digger, and who is now being compared to Dostoievski, Theodore Dreiser and John Steinbeck. . . . He did so much fighting, lying, stealing and school-cutting that he was sent back to his grandmother, who said he would end on the gallows. . . . Then he was put into a Seventh Day Adventist school that was taught by his aunt. It didn't help much, though, and when he was beaten he got a razor and said that he'd cut the next person who beat him" ("Negro Hailed as New Writer"). Five years after the publication of *Native Son*, the *New York Post* reminded readers that Wright, "one of the country's most brilliant young writers and a leading fighter for his race," had been a "juvenile delinquent" and a "chronic drunkard" at the age of six (Braggiotti, 57).

Wright's depiction as both a redeemed Bigger and an insightful, self-educated social critic gives his novel a kind of double credibility. On the one hand, Wright speaks from inside the trap that society has set for people like himself. He has lived in the Jim Crow South and in the overcrowded kitchenette apartments of the North's urban ghettoes. On the other hand, he speaks also as a social scientist and a social worker, the author of a kind of fictional ethnography. This dual status makes Wright an idealized version of the "participant observer" so valued in the cultural studies of the period. He is not an outsider immersing himself in the Black Belt culture to learn about it but an insider who has educated himself and is thus able to speak credibly on behalf of his less eloquent peers.

Native Son establishes its credibility so successfully that early critics often seem to value the novel as much for its sociology as for its literary merits. Keneth Kinnamon's "How *Native Son* was Born" identifies numerous articles and essays from the period that use the novel as a kind of sociological treatise in discussions of residential segregation and crime. In addition, Kinnamon quotes one writer's claim that the novel should be required reading for all judges, prosecutors, and police officers. When Horace R. Cayton reviewed Wright's nonfictional *Twelve Million Black Voices: A Folk History of the Negro in the United States* (1941), he also paid tribute to the social realism of *Native Son*: "With my associates in Sociology and Social Anthropology I studied the social, economic, and psychological background which produced Bigger Thomas of *Native Son*. For every adjective which Wright used we have a label, for every move that Bigger took, we have a map; for every personality type he encountered we have a life history. What I am trying to get over is the fact that in general a large research project which was carried on in Chicago's Black Belt for a period of four years substantiated the entire thesis of *Native Son*" (26).

Cayton does not advance this thesis, but he depicts Wright's work as an elaborate narrative accounting of the deterministic forces that produce, and will continue to produce, personalities like Bigger's. Max makes Bigger's status as the puppet of his environment the cornerstone of his plea that Bigger's life be spared: "Every time he comes in contact with us, he kills! It is a physiological and psychological reaction, embedded in his being. Every thought he thinks is potential murder" (466).

The suggestion that killing has become a "physiological and psychological reaction" for Bigger reflects not only social and cultural determinism of the sort that characterizes *An American Tragedy* but also the language and logic of behaviorism as popularized by B. F. Skinner. In *The Behavior of Organisms* (1938), Skinner notes that the term "conditioned" has passed into the public vocabulary and argues for the usefulness of a distinction between "inborn reflexes" and "acquired reflexes" (61). The terminology is significant because it suggests that learned behavior can take on the thoughtless, instantaneous qualities of reflex. Because Bigger's killing of Mary is both physiological and psychological, it can be presented as determined by environmental conditioning and yet lacking in conscious intent: "Though he had killed by accident, not once did he feel the need to tell himself that it had been an accident. . . . And in a certain sense he knew that the girl's death had not been accidental. He had killed many times before, only on those other times there had been no handy victim or circumstance to make visible or dramatic his will to kill" (119).

The logic and rhetoric of behaviorism also permeates "How 'Bigger' was Born," Wright's 1941 account of the composition of *Native Son*. Wright explains that he saw himself as a "scientist in a laboratory," placing Bigger in "test-tube situations" and recording his responses (523). Early in the article, several real-life models for Bigger are described, and the process that produced these men is labeled "the Bigger Thomas conditioning" (513). Wright argues that although the environment does not create consciousness, "environment supplies the instrumentalities through which the organism expresses itself, and if that environment is warped or tranquil, the mode and manner of behavior will be affected toward deadlocking tensions or orderly fulfillment and satisfaction" (516–17).

The environment of *Native Son* is warped by racial segregation and oppression, by stark and extreme contrasts between the black world and the white. "Because the blacks were so *close* to the very civilization that sought to keep them out, because they could not *help* but react in some way to its incentives and prizes, and because the very tissue of their consciousness received its tone and timbre from the strivings of that dominant civilization, oppression spawned among them a variety of reactions, reaching from outright blind rebellion to a sweet, other-worldly submissiveness" ("How Bigger Was Born,"

511–12). The novel also suggests that the warped environment of segregation can create a different kind of blindness in its white characters; Max, for example, argues that Mary has been "conditioned so that she would regard Bigger Thomas as a kind of beast" (462).

In mapping the forces that influence its characters, *Native Son* is especially sensitive to popular culture and popular narrative, and in this sense the determinism of the novel is less environmental than rhetorical. By quoting from newspaper coverage of Bigger's story—coverage sharply at odds with the reader's own knowledge—the novel demonstrates that Bigger's fate is determined less by the reality of his life than by the stories told about him. The press and the police, for example, force Bigger to participate in the creation of a distorted and sensationalized version of his story. They first take him to Mary Dalton's room so that the rape and the murder can be reenacted for photographers. Bigger refuses to cooperate, but in his resistance he gives the photographers the very picture they seek: "The flashlights went off and he knew in the instant of their flashing that they had taken his picture with his back against a wall, his teeth bared in a snarl" (389). Pictures like this one and stories characterizing Bigger as a feebleminded sex beast generate a public clamor for Bigger's death loud enough to give the proceedings the atmosphere of a lynch mob. The prosecutor, who seeks a death sentence for Bigger, proclaims that "the masses of the citizens who elected him to office" are "standing literally at his back, waiting for him to enforce the law" (433).

Sensationalized press coverage not only argues for Bigger's execution but also gives him a script and a survival handbook to follow during the time between Mary's death and his own. To dispose of a body, tamper with evidence, or collect ransom, Bigger calls not upon experience but upon the practical lessons of formulaic crime melodrama. When he must concoct his own story about the night of Mary's death, the same source tells him what his story must do: "Fingerprints! He had read about them in magazines. His fingerprints would give him away, surely! They could prove that he had been inside of her room. But suppose he told them that he had come to get the trunk? That was it! The *trunk*! His fingerprints had a right to be here" (101).

Bigger seems especially drawn to stories that not only provide practical information but also glamorize crime or otherwise invest it with transcendent meaning. Like the antagonist of so many depression-era crime stories, Bigger identifies in the life of crime an accessible route to wealth and power. When the novel opens, he is a small-time juvenile delinquent whose knowledge of the criminal life is drawn more from ten-cent true crime magazines than from experience. After Mary's death, Bigger begins to envision new freedom. He initially imagines maintaining the facade of normalcy to cloak his more meaningful private life, like a comic-book villain with a secret identity: "Now that the ice was broken, could he not do other things? What was there to stop him? While sitting there at the table awaiting his breakfast, he felt that he was arriving at something that had long eluded him. Things were becoming clear; he would know how to act from now on. The thing to do was to act just like others acted, live like they lived, and while they were not looking, do what you wanted. . . . Now, who on earth would think that he, a black timid negro boy, would murder and burn a rich white girl and would sit and wait for his breakfast like this? Elation filled him" (120).

His elation is later supplanted by a fatalistic determination to go out in glory with a crime spree. Spectacular endings were common in crime stories of the day, most of which followed the formula suggested by the title of a popular comic-book series, *Crime Does Not Pay*. Although the series promised true stories, its offerings always followed a generic, formulaic plot: "By the third page of the lead story, the criminal is an adult and usually an alumnus of reform school or early prison term. He has not learned from his mistakes, however, and returns to a life of more desperate crime. He has a girlfriend or a gang and at least one murder under his belt. He grows cocky and believes that he can beat the law and escape punishment. Through pride, greed, stupidity, or misfortune, however, he is caught, killed, or punished. The last panel of the story, with the criminal dead or facing execution, reminds readers that 'CRIME DOES NOT PAY!' " (Benton, 25).

For Bigger, however, crime ultimately does pay. Criminal acts inspire his first feelings of self-control and self-determination: "And, yet, out of it all, over and above all that had happened, impalpable but real, there remained to him a queer sense of power. *He* had done this. *He* had brought all this about. In all his life these two murders were the most meaningful things that had ever happened to him. He was living, truly and deeply, no matter what others might think, looking at him with their blind eyes. Never had he had the chance to live out the consequences of his actions; never had his will been so free as in this night and day of fear and murder and flight" (277).

Stories, then, are a deterministic force in *Native Son*, exerting a powerful influence over the way characters think, act, and see the world. To understand and possibly to resist stories of such power the reader needs something akin to literary interpretation. Wright credits the labor movement with having opened his eyes to the political agenda that lies beneath the surface of allegedly apolitical writing and also with having taught him strategies for resistant reading. Such reading eventually led Wright to "the pivot of my life": the startling conclusion that all Bigger Thomases were not black ("How Bigger Was Born," 514). After reaching this conclusion, he felt "as though I had put on a pair of spectacles whose power was that of an x-ray enabling me to see deeper into the lives of men. Whenever I picked up a newspaper, I'd no longer feel that I was reading of the doings of whites alone (Negroes are rarely mentioned in the press unless they've committed some crime!), but of a complex struggle for life going on in my country, a struggle in which I was involved" (514–15).

Wright's newfound approach to reading assumes that discourse influences the exercise of power and that discourse need not be straightforward or even fully comprehended in order to be influential. Even in purportedly journalistic and scientific writings, Wright sees a dangerous confusion of fact and fiction. He finds ample illustration of the power of myth in the nation's discussion of race: "The history of the negro is a subject of debate among scientists and anthropologists. The Negro personality is interpreted from a thousand different points of view by different sociologists. Some say that the negro is childish, lazy, etc. These ideas find their way in one form or another even into textbooks taught in public schools. All of this lays a heavy responsibility upon the Negro writer; he cannot trust the so-called experts in history or science, for all too often they are trying to justify the nation's attitude toward the Negro rather than give the truth" (Seaver, 47). The duplicity that characterizes much of the public discussion of race originates, according to Wright, in the nation's willingness, even eagerness, to tolerate lies about slavery. By writing and telling stories about race, the slaveholders spin "tight ideological webs of their right to domination" (Wright, *Twelve Million Black Voices*, 16).

In one sense, then, Wright's novel is an exercise in disentangling the web of ideology, especially as it is manifested in popular narrative. Because the ideology in question is an oppressive one, the novel also attempts to describe as precisely as possible the mechanisms by which ideology shapes power. The criminal justice system provides Wright with the most unambiguous examples of the process at work. He depicts this system as the nation's primary instrument of racial oppression in the years after slavery. Even when the statutes of the penal code disallow racial discrimination—and in 1940 they seldom did—Wright shows that the racist myths are powerful enough to make the criminal justice system take up the work of racial oppression.

The Leopold and Loeb case may have provided Wright with valuable source material for his novel, but it had little to say about race. Wright did not need to look far, however, to find more directly relevant examples. One of the most notorious cases involving race and capital punishment in the thirties came to be known as the Scottsboro case. Jan mentions this case during the awkward dinner scene with Mary and Bigger, in an unsuccessful effort to convince Bigger that the Communists are on the side of African-Americans (85).

The "Scottsboro Boys," as they were often called, were nine black youths, aged thirteen to nineteen, accused of raping two white women while traveling by train from Chattanooga, Tennessee, to Huntsville, Alabama. The nine were arrested on March 25, 1931, the day of the alleged crime. Within two weeks, all but the youngest—thirteen-year-old Roy Wright—had been convicted and sentenced to death. Roy's case ended in mistrial when some jurors refused to follow the prosecution's recommendation, based on the defendant's age, that he be sentenced to life imprisonment. The mistrial was declared when it became clear that the jurors would vote only for death.

In March 1932 the Alabama Supreme Court reversed the conviction of Eugene Williams, another defendant, because of his youth. In the same year the U.S. Supreme Court reversed the convictions of the remaining seven defendants.

The state of Alabama chose to retry all of the men, although Ruby Bates, one of the alleged victims, had recanted her story and testified that the rape allegations had been utterly fabricated. According to Bates, she and Victoria Price (a friend) had illegally boarded the freight train in Chattanooga along with the defendants and another group of white youths. All of the young people were unemployed, and they apparently hoped to find work in Alabama. A fight erupted between the black youths and the white ones. Eventually all but one of the white males were thrown from the slow-moving train. Some of the youths notified the authorities. A large crowd of white police officers and civilians stopped the train near Scottsboro, Alabama. Price and Bates were discovered trying to leave the scene. Within moments the story of a vicious gang rape had begun to circulate through the crowd. Whether the rape allegations originated with Price and Bates or were suggested by the local authorities is unclear, but they were readily accepted.

Even before Ruby Bates changed her testimony, the Scottsboro case had attracted attention around the nation and throughout the world. After she recanted, the case grew in notoriety with astonishing speed. The National Association for the Advancement of Colored People (NAACP) entered into a public and sometimes acrimonious dispute with the Communist Party's International Labor Defense over the right to represent the accused. After six months of wrangling, the NAACP withdrew, apparently in deference to the wishes of the defendants and their families. Thousands attended protest marches in the major cities of the North, and thousands voiced outrage at the protests. The governor of Alabama received an unsolicited letter from Atlanta attorney Earl Sims describing protests that he had witnessed in Switzerland, France, Germany, and Spain. Sims, careful to identify himself as the son of a Confederate veteran and "neither a nigger lover nor a communist," expressed concern that imposing the death penalty on children might make Alabama look uncivilized in the eyes of the world (quoted in Goodman, 59). After years of trials, reversals,

retrials, and commuted sentences, the state of Alabama gave up trying to execute the men. Eventually charges against four of them were
dropped; the others were paroled or escaped. In 1976, Clarence Norris, one of the defendants, was pardoned. All nine served at least six
years in prison. One was jailed for nineteen.

The Scottsboro story unfolded in the national press throughout the
thirties, at a time when Wright was involved in both the Communist
Party and the composition of *Native Son*. The case is relevant to *Native
Son* because it deals with racial bias in the courts, with the use of the
criminal justice system to perform a kind of lynching, and with the
defense by Communists of African-Americans in capital cases. By
telling the public that accusations of rape—even incredible, recanted
accusations—were always believed in cases involving black men and
white women, the Scottsboro case also validated Bigger's assumption
that no one would believe the true story of Mary's death. The Scottsboro defendants, like Bigger, were guilty because the crime of which
they were accused, according to the mythology, exactly expresses the
essence of their beings. A Birmingham resident succinctly voiced this
belief about African-American men in a letter about the Scottsboro
trial that appeared in the *Birmingham News*: "His conception of law is
a policeman's club, and his idea of liberty is license; basically he is a
human negation. His idea of civilization is limited by something he
can get into his mouth. Sex is the dominating quality of his makeup
and he can no more help it than can a monkey or an African Gorilla"
(quoted in Goodman, 116).

Bigger differs from the Scottsboro defendants, of course, in that he
is guilty. The distinction, however, is not as straightforward as it
might appear. Bigger does not rape and murder Mary, but he is executed for doing so. He recognizes that "when they killed him it would
be for Mary's death, not Bessie's" (351). Like the Scottsboro defendants, Bigger is presented to the public in a biography that presumes
his guilt. In the press and therefore in the eyes of many prospective
jurors, Bigger is not only guilty of raping and murdering a defenseless
white girl but is a "black ape" who was driven by instinct to commit
the crime. Such language even finds its way into the courtroom as a
part of the prosecution's summation: "The law is strong and gracious
enough to allow all of us to sit her in this courtroom today and try

this case with dispassionate interest, and not tremble with fear that at this very moment some half-human black ape may be climbing through the windows of our homes to rape, murder, and burn our daughters!" (475–76).

Bigger may be framed for raping and murdering Mary, but Wright does not give readers the tragic tale of an innocent boy executed. If any one section in *Native Son* marks the point at which it breaks away from *An American Tragedy*, it is the scene of Bessie's murder. When Bigger kills Mary, he does so accidentally and without even the sort of ambiguity that surrounds Clyde Griffiths's role in the death of Roberta Alden. When he carries out his plan to eliminate Bessie by bludgeoning her and dropping her down an elevator shaft, however, there is no doubt that he has committed cold-blooded murder.

The case that seems most to have influenced Wright's depiction of Bigger after Bessie's murder is the Robert Nixon case. In "How 'Bigger' Was Born," Wright explains, "when I was halfway through the first draft of *Native Son* a case paralleling Bigger's flared forth in the newspapers of Chicago. (Many of the newspaper items and some of the incidents in *Native Son* are but fictionalized versions of the Robert Nixon case and rewrites of news stories from the Chicago Tribune.)" (532). Margaret Walker reports that Wright followed the Nixon case enthusiastically. He wrote to her in Chicago (he was living in New York at the time) and requested that she collect all newspaper reports on the case. For about a year she saved every article on the case from each of Chicago's five daily papers. Wright "would spread [the clippings] all out and read them over and over again and then take off from there in his own imagination" (123). Walker also reports that Wright traveled to Chicago and visited Ulysses S. Keys, Nixon's first attorney. On the day of the visit, Nixon's family had removed Keys from the case and had replaced him with a lawyer hired by the NAACP. When Keys complained about being dismissed after writing a brief on the case, Walker asked for and received permission for Wright to use the brief in his research.

The Nixon case is evident more in Wright's depiction of public reaction to Bigger's crimes than in the novel's plot. Nixon and Earl Hicks were accused of beating a white woman to death with a brick during a botched robbery. The case had been highly sensationalized in the

Chicago press. As with Bigger, newspaper stories proclaimed, with no evidence, that the woman had been raped. Authorities also made allegations, never substantiated, that Nixon was responsible for a number of other murders. In print he was called a "brick moron," a "giant ape," a "jungle man," and an "earlier link in the species" (quoted in Kinnamon, 113). Nixon was executed in 1938.

Bigger is often called a black ape in the novel, and the plot—which bears little resemblance to the Leopold and Loeb, Scottsboro, or Nixon cases—unfolds in ironic counterpoint to one of the era's most popular films, *King Kong* (1931). Like Kong, Bigger is transplanted from his native surroundings—the Black Belt—into a glittering, unfamiliar world where he develops a disastrous sexual attraction for a beautiful white woman. When Bigger flees, he triggers a massive manhunt and proves himself willing to murder rather than be captured. At the end of his flight, driven by a desperation that seems born of instinct rather than intellect, Bigger climbs—first to the top of a tall building, then to the top of a tower that sits atop the building. He is surrounded, shot at, and eventually blasted from his perch.

King Kong has often been read as an allegory about white America's fear of its black population. Its plot parallels *Native Son*'s in a way that accommodates this interpretation. Both novel and film appeared at a time when newspapers could describe African-Americans as apes or as apelike. As Keneth Kinnamon establishes in "How *Native Son* was Born," the openly racist fragments of newspaper reports that Wright includes in the novel are not exaggerated fabrications but quotations almost verbatim from articles about Nixon that appeared in the *Chicago Tribune*. One report states that Nixon's "physical characteristics suggest an earlier link in the species" and declares that Nixon killed "with a ferocity suggestive of Poe's 'Murder in the Rue Morgue'—the work of a giant ape" (quoted in Kinnamon, 113–14). Wright's novel shows that Bigger's life story can easily be refashioned into a racist myth, but the novel's title suggests that Bigger, murderer or not, is a true American.

As the Scottsboro and Nixon cases show, the criminal justice system allows myths about race to influence the outcome of an individual defendant's trial. *Native Son*, however, is concerned also with the influence of these myths on the population at large. Through mythic discourse, elements of slavery live on even after the supporting infra-structure of statutory authority has been removed. In a 1940 inter-view in the Mexican magazine *Romance*, Wright spoke to this aspect of American society. He stated that African-Americans "still live in conditions very similar to slavery" (Wright, "A Conversation," 32). Bigger's story shows the image of the monstrous capital offender being used to justify and to manage the police and civilian power that maintains these conditions: "Though he could not have put it into words, he felt that not only had they resolved to put him to death, but that they were determined to make his death mean more than a mere punishment; that they regarded him as a figment of that black world which they feared and were anxious to keep under control. The atmosphere of the crowd told him that they were going to use his death as a bloody symbol of fear to wave before the eyes of that black world" (318–19).

In a literal and immediate sense, Bigger's flight is used to justify sweeping escalations in police power, escalations directed at African-Americans and at the Communists. Max makes this aspect of the case a part of his argument that Bigger's life should be spared: "The authorities of the city and state deliberately inflamed the public mind to the point where they could not keep the peace without martial law. . . . The hunt for Bigger Thomas served as an excuse to terrorize the entire Negro population, to arrest hundreds of communists, to raid labor union headquarters and workers' organizations. Indeed, the tone of the press, the silence of the church, the attitude of the prose-cution and the stimulated temper of the people are of such a nature as to indicate that *more* than revenge is being sought upon a man who has committed a crime" (448).

If punishing criminals like Bigger also provides the force and au-thority used to maintain conditions "very similar to slavery" in the years after emancipation, the novel also demonstrates that physical force is not needed when ideological force is strong enough, when myths and stories persuade enough people to do the work of racial oppression. Wright suggests that power in modern society is exer-cised and shaped largely through discourse. By charting the links be-tween the two, he establishes a rhetoric of power.

Wright notes that oppression can adopt the voice and tone of paternal kindness. In *Twelve Million Black Voices*, he argues that, in order to obscure problems of race relations and soothe a guilty conscience, the United States has evolved a system "of brutal kindness, of genial despotism" (16). Bigger may seethe with unfocused rage and fear, but when he comes face to face with white people in the novel, they are likely to smile, shake his hand, give him a job, or even take him to dinner. The benevolent demeanor of characters such as Mr. Dalton suggests that the relationship between power and discourse is not a straightforward one. A grim, predatory determinism guides Mr. Dalton's actions, but his rhetoric is warm and generous, tough but fair. This sort of rhetoric allows for the openly oppressive power of the Old South to be replicated nationwide in subtle, unofficial forms.

Wright's approach to reading popular culture allows him to see a political power play even in apparently positive racial stereotypes: "There's something serious to be said about this legend that all Negroes are kind and love animals and children. . . . That legend . . . serves to protect certain guilt feelings about the Negro. If you can feel that he is so different that he is just naturally happy and he smiles automatically you kind of exclude him, in an ironic sense, from the human race and therefore you don't have to treat him exactly like you would treat other people and you don't have to feel bad about mistreating him" ("How Richard Wright Looks at *Black Boy*," *Conversations*, 65). By depicting the Daltons as self-deluded progressives, Wright shows that the rhetoric of crime and punishment persuades not only through dehumanization but also by flattering those in power and inspiring their righteous indignation. The fact that the Daltons see themselves as philanthropists and "negrophiles" makes Bigger's crimes against them all the more monstrous. Only a beast or an unrepentant fiend would commmit so loathsome a crime after receiving so many gifts, so many handouts. The more progressive the Daltons are, and the more sympathetic to Bigger's "people," the more his crime merits death.

In Wright's portrayal, the Daltons are simultaneously blinded and guided by myth. Mr. Dalton's vision of the world is in some ways no more acute than Bigger's or even Mrs. Dalton's. He seems sincere but oblivious to his own hypocrisy and to his own critical role in residential segregation, a practice characterized in the novel as the cornerstone of American apartheid. On the witness stand, Mr. Dalton concedes that his company charges higher rent to black families than white ones for comparable housing. He also asserts that rent rates are determined by "the law of supply and demand" (377). When pressed to explain why he rents to blacks only inside the Black Belt, Dalton explains, "I—I—I don't think they'd like to live any other place. . . . I think Negroes are happier when they're together" (378). The novel thus suggests that the myths surrounding race and power can dazzle rich as well as poor. It may take Jim Crow laws, lynchings, and segregation to sustain the family fortune, but Mr. Dalton's self-deception is so complete that he can, apparently without qualms, consider himself a philanthropist when one of the tenants he restricts to an overpriced kitchenette apartment is hired as his chauffeur.

Blindness keeps Mr. Dalton the slumlord unaware of both the degree to which he benefits from racial oppression and the extent to which his livelihood depends on crime. Companies like his own compel African-Americans to live in the most benighted areas, then charge them more rent than whites pay for larger apartments. Likewise, stores in black neighborhoods, few of which are owned by blacks, charge more for food than whites pay in whites-only stores a few blocks away. Such conditions not only exploit the black population economically but also, according to Wright, produce crime in some young men like Bigger. As a result a substantial portion of black men find themselves caught up in the criminal justice system at an early age. For the black community, the consequence is more sons and fathers in jail, more single parent homes, and more men who, when released from incarceration, find themselves unable, as ex-cons, to get the kind of work that supports families. It means that men like Bigger will periodically be driven to robbery and murder, increasing the need for police and vigilante forces, forces that can also be used to maintain segregation.

Another characteristic of the discourse of racial oppression in the novel is its tendency to exaggerate differences between groups of people and thus to widen the gaps between white and black, rich and poor, normal and criminal. Bigger is dehumanized and characterized as an ape, while Mr. Dalton is ennobled as a high-minded "friend of the Negro." The novel undermines this polarizing rhetoric by suggesting that characters like Bigger, Jan, and the Daltons are in fact more similar than different. Max tells Bigger that "the people who hate you feel just as you feel, only they're on the other side of the fence. . . . They want the things of life, just as you did, and they're not particular about how they get them" (499–500). We see that Mary and Jan are not unlike Bigger and Bessie—they all enjoy drinking and sex, they all are drawn to glamour and wealth, and they all defy authority.

Mary and Jan, despite their declared good intentions, are also capable of dehumanizing people like Bigger, just as Bigger is capable of dehumanizing his victims. They can congratulate themselves for treating Bigger as an equal, and for dining with him and sitting beside him in the car, but when a romantic mood strikes, they retire to the back seat, utterly indifferent to the servant's presence. There is even a kind of symmetry between Mr. Dalton and Bigger: Bigger is willing to commit murder if he can get away with the ransom money, and Mr. Dalton rents squalid one-room apartments in "blacks only" buildings at rates kept artificially high through residential segregation.

Although Bigger is presented as a pawn of forces, rhetorical and otherwise, that overwhelm him, these forces do not make him a cold-blooded killer or a hardened desperado, at least not until well after the first, accidental killing. Bigger does not kill Mary to conceal a rape, to strike back at the living symbol of his oppression (at least not consciously), or even as part of a foiled ransom scheme. He kills her by accident, panic-stricken at the thought of being discovered in her bedroom. Bigger's willingness to assume the role of murderer nevertheless is perhaps best understood as his unwillingness to have people know the truth—namely that a blind woman and her semiconscious teenage daughter frightened him so much that he *accidentally* killed one of them. To acknowledge this truth is to concede that he walks in terror in the white world, that he is unable to control his actions or foresee their consequences. Bigger would rather be seen as a diabolical, cold-blooded murderer and rapist than as the scared, bungling servant and small-time hood that he is.

After taking on the role of cold-blooded killer, Bigger feels more confident and is more self-aware: "He felt that he had his destiny in his grasp. He was more alive than he could ever remember having been; his mind and attention were pointed, focused toward a goal" (170). In part he has tapped into the aura of power surrounding the folkloric figure of the outlaw, but Bigger is ultimately drawn not by the lure of crime but by the promise of choice: "He could run away; he could remain; he could even go down and confess what he had done. The mere thought that these avenues of action were open to him made him feel free, that his life was his, that he held his future in his hands" (218).

Bigger's sense of autonomy in the hours and days after Mary's death, however, is eventually revealed as self-delusion. He can hatch elaborate plans for his story and for the ransom but is unable to dispose of the body. Like Leopold and Loeb, Bigger dreams of the perfectly planned crime even as he makes one elementary error after another. The delusional element is also evident from the degree to which Bigger's vision of himself is shaped by grade B movies, men's magazines, and pulp fiction. Even passages devoted to describing Bigger's newfound self-awareness often reveal that the "reality" he now sees so sharply is rooted in mass-market, escapist fantasy: "For the first time in his life he moved consciously between two sharply defined poles: he was moving away from the threatening penalty of death, from the death-like times that brought him that tightness and hotness in his chest; and he was moving toward that sense of fulness he had so often but inadequately felt in magazines and movies" (170).

Bigger seeks out the role of outlaw murderer, about which he has learned from magazines and movies, and begins to play it even before he has actually murdered. This role equips Bigger with strategies for living on the run and makes him willing to do anything necessary to remain at large. He presents his decision to kill Bessie, for example, in the language of a hard-boiled villain: "Coldly, he knew that he had to take her with him, and then at some future time settle things with her, settle them in a way that would not leave him in any danger." This is the voice of cold-blooded self-interest, but it yields in the next sentence to the suggestion that Bigger acts not in accordance with his own desires but as if spellbound: "He thought of it calmly, as if the decision were being handed down to him by some logic not his own, over which he had no control, but which he had to obey" (264). The power that this logic exerts over Bigger demonstrates that discourse can be a deterministic force without being overtly oppressive and without characterizing people as subhuman or as born murderers. Bigger's actions in the novel are influenced much more by the mythic role that he strives to play than by the stereotyped images used to dehumanize him in the press and in the courtroom.

Max argues that Bigger's crimes are born of an unbearable tension originating in the glamorous life that is always before his eyes but always out of reach. "Your honor, consider the mere physical aspect of our civilization. How alluring, how dazzling it is! How it excites the senses! How it seems to dangle within easy reach of everyone the fulfillment of happiness! How constantly and overwhelmingly the advertisements, radios, newspapers and movies play upon us! But in thinking of them remember that to many they are tokens of mockery. . . . Imagine a man walking amid such a scene, a part of it, and yet knowing that it is *not* for him!" (459). Bigger has been conditioned to desire a particular reward. He is forced to live within reach of that reward while simultaneously being forbidden to touch it.

Although sheer terror drives him to kill Mary without even being aware that he is doing so, afterward Bigger believes "that he had been in the grip of a weird spell and was now free" (99). Almost immediately, this newfound freedom leads him toward more crime and ultimately toward the Big Score: the ransom money. "Here he was sitting with them, and they did not know that he had murdered a white girl and cut her head off and burnt her body. The thought of what he had done, the awful horror of it, the daring associated with such actions, formed for him for the first time in his fear-ridden life a barrier of protection between him and a world he feared. He had murdered and had created a new life for himself. . . . His crime was an anchor weighing him safely in time; it added to him a certain confidence which his gun and knife did not" (119).

Bigger may gain more confidence from his crime than from his weapons. When he thinks to himself that he has "murdered a white girl," however, he reveals just how thoroughly he has rewritten his own story. When he accepts the fiction that he is a murderer and an outlaw, he sees himself entering into a desperate battle with the forces that sought to oppress him and to restrict him to a life of servitude. When he begins to act on this premise, however, he accomplishes little in the way of effective resistance and much that might further the cause of racial oppression. Proclaiming himself murderer of a "white girl," Bigger in fact murders only Bessie. He fails in his attempts to outwit the police and to extort money from the Daltons but succeeds in having martial law declared in the Black Belt. The newspapers report that the search for Bigger involves five thousand police officers and three thousand "volunteers" and also that "several Negro men were beaten in North and West Side neighborhoods." Because of hysteria over the danger Bigger represents, "several hundred Negroes resembling Bigger Thomas were rounded up from South Side 'hot spots,' " and hundreds of other African-Americans are dismissed from their jobs (282–83).

Bigger's decision to play the role of cold-blooded killer makes him, ironically, a tool of racial oppression. Bigger eventually rejects this role, however, and undergoes a second transformation: "Out of the mood of renunciation there sprang up in him again the will to kill. But this time it was not directed outward toward people, but inward, upon himself. Why not kill that wayward yearning within him that had led him to this end? He had reached out and killed and had not solved anything, so why not reach inward and kill that which had duped him? This feeling sprang up of itself, organically, automatically; like the rotted hull of a seed forming the soil in which it should grow again" (316–17). Bigger's need, late in the novel, to confess and to explain might also be taken as a sign of his transformation, a sign that he is beginning to come to grips with and take responsibility for his actions. "He would have gladly admitted his guilt if he thought that in doing so he could have also given in the same breath a sense of the deep, choking hate that had been his life, a hate that he had not wanted to have, but could not help having. How could he do that? The impulsion to try to tell was as deep as had been the urge to kill" (356).

Bigger does not have the chance to develop a political consciousness, but the novel ends by suggesting that he is moving in that direction at the time of his execution. He is able, for example, to address Jan by his given name rather than as "Mr. Jan." Wright seems to find in the Communist experience a political alternative to the rebellious-ness that might otherwise find an outlet in crime. Jan, like Bigger, is from a criminalized group that has been represented in the popular media as a threat to the very fabric of society. Bigger knows almost nothing about communism when the novel opens, but he "remem-bered seeing many cartoons of communists in newspapers and al-ways they had flaming torches in their hands and wore beards and were trying to commit murder or set things on fire" (74).

Perhaps Wright intends Jan and the other Communists to be mod-els for resistant political action by African-Americans. Unlike Bigger, Jan knows how to stand up for himself against the police; he does not respond to threats, and he seeks out Bigger on his own in order to learn the truth. Later, sensing that his release from jail is some kind of trick, Jan refuses to leave. Bigger's flight is characterized by newfound feelings of self-determination and self-control that are ul-timately shown to be ephemeral. Jan and the Communists seek the same things in a way that is not pathological, egoistic, and criminal but collective and political. Ultimately the fact that Bigger undergoes at least the beginnings of a positive transformation is a refutation of biological determinism. Even within the hostile environment of the prison, Bigger's experiences and acknowledgment of his humanity combine to improve him and thus to demonstrate the essential plas-ticity of his personality.

In "How Bigger Was Born," Wright lists several originals for Big-ger. Bigger Number One is utterly unsympathetic, a stereotype of the child bully. Number Two expresses his contempt for whites and for Jim Crow laws by refusing to pay his bills and his rent. According to Wright, Number Two acts out feelings shared by many African-Americans too cautious or too morally restrained to follow suit and "was in prison the last time I heard from him" (508). Number Three was "what the white folks called a 'bad nigger,' " hated by both blacks and whites. Number Four was shot dead while delivering boot-leg liquor. Number Four openly flouts Jim Crow laws while oscillating wildly between depression and elation. He is bookish, jobless, and eventually "sent to an asylum for the insane" (509). Number Five is a man "who always rode the Jim Crow streetcars without paying and sat wherever he pleased" (509). Wright claims to have seen Number

Five sit in the white seats on a streetcar and calmly flash a knife at the conductor who had ordered him to move. The threat of violence intimidates the crew and the white passengers into muttering inaction while amusing and secretly satisfying the other black passengers. Wright says, "I don't know what happened to Bigger No. 5. But I can guess" (509).

These prototypes are united not by the specific nature of their crimes but by the forces that produce their personality type. It is a type characterized by volatile intractability, especially in the areas of law and race: "The Bigger Thomases were the only Negroes I know of who consistently violated the Jim Crow laws of the South and got away with it, at least for a sweet brief spell" (509). Bigger Thomas, far from being unique, is a type with exemplars and thus demonstrably the product of deterministic forces. Here, according to Max, is reason enough to spare Bigger's life. Max argues that the forces that make Bigger murderous are so powerful that he is helpless to resist them: "Every movement of his body is an unconscious protest. Every desire, every dream, no matter how intimate or personal, is a plot or a conspiracy. Every hope is a plan for insurrection. Every glance of the eye is a threat. *His very existence is a crime against the state!*" (466). This argument seems grounded in assumptions about personal responsibility that are common to many literary treatments of determinism, especially in the naturalist novel. Wright depicts a society that mechanically, inevitably, produces homicidal young men like Bigger, men willing to be executed as condemned murderers and rapists for the sake of a "sweet brief spell" of freedom and self-determination. Because the social structure produces the crimes, the individual perpetrator has diminished responsibility.

Max's strategy also opens the door, however, to the more sinister implications of determinism and criminal responsibility that characterize diagnostic biography. By proving that Bigger could not help but kill, Max also proves that Bigger can never be trusted not to kill, that he is inherently murderous. Within the diagnostic biography of the capital offender, the implications of such innate dangerousness are all too clear. For Bigger and those like him, any freedom gained through transgression creates a considerable and unforgivable debt: "Eventually," according to Wright, "the Whites who restricted their lives made them pay a terrible price. They were shot, hanged, maimed, lynched, and generally hounded until they were either dead or their spirits broken" (509–10). Like *An American Tragedy, Native Son* identifies the antecedents of a capital crime. By doing so novels associate danger with the poor and with those who depart from strict standards of normalcy and decency. Bigger and Clyde are both born to urban poverty. Both are drawn away from their unstable families and into a criminalized peer group while in their midteens. Both are also exposed while still young to petty crime, alcohol, carousing, and promiscuity.

Bigger is like Clyde Griffiths in his deviation from accepted behavioral standards, in his lower-class origins, and in his involvement with a seedy juvenile subculture. Unlike Clyde, however, Bigger has no hope of becoming, or of marrying, a member of the wealthy elite. Bigger is part of a race that, according to the prevailing mythology, embodies the indecent, the abnormal, and the psychopathic. This mythology and the social structure supported by it are the most powerful determinants of Bigger's life and crimes. Because of his race, he is forced to live in poverty, to hope for a job as a servant, and to adopt a posture of slouching, shuffling humility in the presence of any white person. Overwhelmed by stress, he accidentally suffocates Mary, and his race ensures that he will be executed for the killing. When the knowledge that he is doomed prompts Bigger to evade punishment, the fact that he is black and his alleged victim white means that thousands of white people participate in a manhunt terrorizing thousands of African-Americans.

Contradictory interpretations of determinism, then, call into question the status of *Native Son* as a protest novel. In the course of voicing its protest, the novel proposes a model for understanding the effect of social structure on an individual's behavior. If the model is found credible, and it has often been, then there are two possible responses, two ways in which society may react. One is to end all racial segregation, whether statutory or customary. Max argues that Bigger's trial can produce such a result by forcing people to reexamine the very fabric of society: "Perhaps it is in a manner fortunate that the defendant has committed one of the darkest crimes in our memory; for if we can encompass the life of this man and find out what has hap-

101

pened to him, if we can understand how subtly and yet strongly his life and fate are linked to ours—if we can do this, perhaps we can find the key to our future, that rare vantage point upon which every man and woman in this nation can stand and view how inextricably our hopes and fears of today create the exultation and doom of tomorrow" (444).

Failing this movement into a more enlightened world, or at least in the meantime, to accept Max's argument is to adopt the view that every encounter between white and black in America is charged with the potential for murder. Max argues that white society has buried African-Americans in urban ghettoes as if it were hiding the corpse of a murder victim. Too late it has been discovered that the corpse is not dead: "It still lives! It has made itself a home in the wild forest of our great cities, amid the rank and choking vegetation of slums! It has forgotten our language! In order to live it has sharpened its claws! It has grown hard and calloused! It has developed a capacity for hate and fury which we cannot understand! . . . By night it creeps from its lair and steals toward the settlements of civilization! And at the sight of a kind face it does not lie down upon its back and kick up its heels playfully to be tickled and stroked. No; it leaps to kill!" (456–57). Max may intend this speech as part of a plea for mercy, but it seems unlikely to hasten desegregation and likely to lead to even harsher police measures. For Wright's white readers, Max's plea means that every black face, whether hostile or friendly, confident or subservient, hides a potential murderer. Such a vision is far more likely to make those in power want to hire more police and build more prisons.

Wright's strategy in part involves intimidation. He suggests not only that U.S. society will continue to produce individual killers like Bigger but also that the society's racist structure will lead, inevitably, to violent, collective insurrection. In "How Bigger Was Born," Wright argues that the "Bigger Thomas" reaction is motivated by the same feelings of alienation, exclusion, and resentment that propelled the Nazis to power. His argument uncannily resembles the one put forth by Robert Lindner, five years later, in *Rebel Without a Cause*; Lindner sees the psychopath as an "embryonic stormtrooper" (16). Wright, of course, is writing in 1940, before the worst Nazi atrocities, but his words would still strike a chord of fear in the hearts of many white

Americans. He also associates the American black population with the Bolsheviks and the Italian fascists. In these cases as well, the strategy is a dangerous one. Even as it calls for sweeping social reform, it increases the aura of danger around African-Americans and thus justifies their further oppression.

Bigger's eager assumption of the intentional, rather than the accidental, interpretation of Mary's killing can likewise be seen as a risky attempt to exploit fear of the monstrous criminal in a bid for power. When Bigger chooses to think of himself as a cold-blooded killer, he reveals an odd parallel between the clinical profile of the psychopath and the folkloric archetype of the hardened criminal. Both are emotionless, entirely self-interested, and dangerous. Both are capable of passing for harmless, law-abiding citizens. Ironically, however, the path that Bigger follows in search of freedom and self-determination provides the evidence needed to show that he deserves to die. He is lured into the role of cold-blooded killer by the promise of power and self-control and by the desire to efface the pathetic true tale of Mary's killing with a horrific tale of diabolical evil personified. Rather than simply tell the truth or flee, Bigger follows a course of action that assures his capture and execution. By burning Mary's body, for example, Bigger incinerates all but the most fundamental physical evidence, creating a void that the other characters in the novel must fill from their own imaginations.

The ambiguity in the message of *Native Son* is perhaps best illustrated when we consider how this message plays out in the courts and in the criminal justice system. On the one hand, Wright voices the criticism of capital punishment that more than any other leads the Supreme Court to impose a moratorium on executions: the death penalty is applied in a racially biased manner. On the other hand, by highlighting the crucial and potentially misleading role of narrative in the criminal justice system—especially in sentencing—Wright shows that the problem is inherent in the system. As long as discretionary sentencing persists, racial bias will be able to find its way into the judicial process. Ultimately, Wright suggests, our criminal justice system is an instrument of racial oppression not because it fails to live up to its mandate but because it expresses the will of the people. The system is as much a part of the nation as Bigger is a native son.

103

I have certainly heard it said that, on occasion he chased with a scythe a child who happened to be in his yard; but people also said that it was only in jest. Certainly no one would have thought anything more of it had it not been for the murders he has committed.

—Testimony of Pierre Riviere's Priest in Foucault's *I, Pierre Riviere*

The power in the hierarchized surveillance of the disciplines is not possessed as a thing, or transferred as a property; it functions like a piece of machinery. . . . This enables the disciplinary power to be both absolutely indiscreet, since it is everywhere and always alert, since by its very principle it leaves no zone of shade . . . and absolutely "discreet," for it functions permanently and largely in silence.

—Foucault, *Discipline*

F I V E

Truman Capote's *In Cold Blood:* The Novel as Prison

In the forty years between *An American Tragedy* and *In Cold Blood*, many of the arguments advanced in Dreiser's novel and in Wright's *Native Son* eventually brought a temporary halt to capital punishment. *An American Tragedy* showed that discretionary sentencing allows class bias and wealth to shape a judge's or jury's perceptions of dangerousness, degree of responsibility and self-control, and punishability. Around the country, and especially in the Deep South, discretionary sentencing permitted all-white juries to sentence African-Americans and the very poor to death while sparing well-to-do whites convicted of the same offenses. This demonstrably inconsistent sentencing and racist bias prompted the U.S. Supreme Court to rule in 1972, in *Furman v. Georgia*, that death sentences were being awarded in a manner so "arbitrary" and "freakish" as to be unconstitutional. There ensued an unofficial moratorium on executions. Capote's novel was published almost exactly at the beginning of a decade in which no death sentences were carried out.

Capote's novel also marks a shift in the kind of capital offender under scrutiny. *McTeague* and *An American Tragedy* depict the sudden and startling eruption of murder in previously law-abiding working-class men. Bigger Thomas is a small-time hood who finds the role of murderer forced upon him. *In Cold Blood* and *The Executioner's Song* depict state-raised convicts, willful delinquents who seem to opt for a criminal, subversive lifestyle. In one sense, the difference reflects a change in the practice of execution. Norris and Dreiser wrote about relatively anonymous offenders at a time when executions were fairly frequent. Patrick Collins and Chester Gillette were unremarkable members of a large crowd, two representative cases chosen from hundreds. Capote and Mailer wrote at a time when executions occurred rarely, if at all. Today the executed few tend to be the most violent hard-core delinquents and convicts, criminals of the sort least suited to the defense mounted by Dreiser and Darrow.

The two murderers at the center of *In Cold Blood* are Perry Smith and Richard Hickock. In mid-November of 1959, Smith, thirty-one, and Hickock, twenty-eight, murdered four members of the Clutter family in the small town of Holcomb, Kansas. The family had operated one of the most prosperous and prominent farms in the area. Herb and Bonnie Clutter had four children, but only the two youngest, sixteen-year-old Nancy and fifteen-year-old Kenyon, still lived at home. Smith and Hickock had recently been released from prison, and Hickock had learned, from an inmate who worked on the Clutter farm years earlier, that the Clutter home contained a hidden safe filled with money.

The two men entered the house in the middle of the night through an unlocked door, roused the four sleepers at gunpoint, bound and gagged them, and left them in four different rooms. After discovering that the house held no safe, and no more than fifty dollars in cash, Smith and Hickock stabbed Herb Clutter, used a shotgun to kill all

In Cold Blood

four, and fled. They remained at large for more than six weeks, even spending time in Mexico, before being captured in Las Vegas. In 1965, Smith and Hickock were hanged, two of seven men executed nation-wide that year.

The Clutter murders attracted a good deal of media attention in the region and even received brief notice in the *New York Times*. When Truman Capote read the notice, he found the subject for his next book. After years of research and writing, including lengthy inter-views with the principal players, Capote published his "nonfiction novel" *In Cold Blood*. The book was a startling success. It sold millions of copies and became the basis for a highly acclaimed feature film. Like *McTeague* and *An American Tragedy*, *In Cold Blood* was inspired by a particular real-life murder case. Capote claimed, however, that his book was not only realistic but scrupulously true. In the book, Capote referred to places and to most people by their true names, and in interviews he claimed to have neither invented nor altered any inci-dent. Capote promoted the book as the first of a new genre, the "non-fiction novel."

In Cold Blood is a retelling of the Clutter murders using the novelis-tic conventions of realism. It is told by a third-person, omniscient narrator, in a style that might be termed documentary. The novel appears to recreate all of the most important scenes in the story— from the murders to the breaks in the investigation to the hangings— and scenes are typically presented with few interruptions and lots of dialogue. During one courtroom scene depicting testimony by psychi-atrist Dr. W. Mitchell Jones, however, there are two curious interrup-tions. The first occurs when Jones is asked if he "has an opinion as to whether or not Richard Eugene Hickock knew right from wrong at the time of the commission of the crime." After replying that "within the usual definitions Mr. Hickock did know right from wrong," he is asked if he can qualify or elaborate that answer (330). The prosecut-ing attorney objects, the objection is sustained, and Dr. Jones is dis-missed from the stand.

Dr. Jones's qualification of his answer is disallowed because, under the M'Naghten Rule, anything beyond a "yes" is irrelevant. At this moment in the narrative, however, something odd occurs. Capote's narrator interrupts the account of the trial to tell us what Dr. Jones would have said, "had [he] been allowed to speak further." In the page or so that follows we read that Hickock is "above average in intelligence," although he "seems incapable of learning from experience." He "professes usual moral standards [but] seems obviously uninfluenced by them in his actions." Finally, Dr. Jones concludes that Hickock should be tested for "organic brain damage" that "might have substantially influenced his behavior during the past several years and at the time of his crime" (330–31).

Dr. Jones is recalled to the stand to testify about Perry Smith, and this time he states that he has no opinion "as to whether or not [Smith] knew right from wrong at the time of the offense involved in this action" (333). Once again any qualification of the answer is disallowed, and once again the narrator interrupts to insert what Jones would have said, "had [he] been permitted to discourse on the cause of his indecision" (333). This time readers hear not only from Dr. Jones but also from Dr. Joseph Satten, who sees Smith as fitting the profile described in an article Satten coauthored, "Murder Without Apparent Motive—A Study in Personality Disorganization."[1]

What prompts the narrative to fill in these "gaps" in the trial? Why not simply recreate the exchange of dialogue? It should be noted that, in interpolating this testimony about psychological motive, the novel may depart somewhat from its own format. Still, it does not depart radically from the format of the trial: Dr. Jones's testimony may be strictly limited, but the court does not restrict its attention to the question of guilt or innocence. Smith and Hickock confess to the crimes before the trial, and they never withdraw these confessions. Their attorneys do not even attempt to argue for acquittal but instead mount a defense based on character witnesses in an attempt to dissuade the jury from the death penalty. By including what Dr. Jones would have said, *In Cold Blood* merely elaborates on and professionalizes this testimony about character.

It would seem, at least in the case of capital crimes, that simple proof of guilt is not enough; execution also requires particular forms of motive. If the motive seems wildly irrational, a product of insanity, the killer will be institutionalized but not executed. If the motive, on

---

[1]Published in the *American Journal of Psychiatry* 117 (July 1960): 48–53.

the other hand, is found to be relatively rational, the killer is also likely to be spared. It becomes most difficult to evaluate motive in the case of monstrous, apparently motiveless crimes committed by someone not clearly insane. The apparent sanity of the accused, in conjunction with the ghastly, incomprehensible nature of his crimes, seems to demand maximal punishment, but the lack of understandable motive suggests mental illness and thus diminished responsibility. Often, the criminal psychologist must unravel the knot. When the only indication of insanity is the "motiveless" crime itself, criminal psychology can provide a motive by decoding the killer's deranged logic and translating the killer's actions into a sensible form. The identification and classification of the criminal behind the crime are generally described as the end results of disinterested observation: the offender, scrutinized by a trained eye, is discovered to be a certain type of individual. But it is hard to sustain this objective stance, as we have seen, particularly in cases involving capital crimes. How can anyone be objective while evaluating the biography of a known killer? Criminal biography, as I have argued, is less a means of determining who the offender is than of constructing the offender as juridical subject. What appears to be mere observation and diagnosis is actually the exercise of power, an act that establishes the complete authority of the criminal justice system over the offender.

In the case of the delinquent or the psychopath, the criminal act is depicted as a manifestation of a criminal personality that lurked beneath the surface all along. No detail about the offender's past, even in an ostensibly journalistic work like *In Cold Blood*, can be "merely" documentary, because even minutiae prefigure moments of apocalyptic violence. The details become clues to the subject's psychopathy, and we see that the offender is no ordinary human but instead a dangerous kind of automaton or monster. This shift from specific crime to individual criminal removes the criminal act from its particular time frame in a way that effectively disguises the exercise of power. The criminal act is extended into the past, and the criminal justice system thus appears to have no part in the production of crime and delinquency: the subject was a criminal personality long before being discovered as one. The criminal act is also extended into a potential future. Incarceration becomes necessary in the interest of public safety.

108

In Cold Blood reproduces the strategies of power associated with modern carceral discourse, "imprisoning" Smith and Hickock within deterministic narratives while simultaneously working to disavow any connection to power. The basis of this disavowal is the term "nonfiction novel," which, as I will show, posits a complete disjunction between the realms of art and power. The novel's omniscient point of view recreates the privileged, diagnostic vision of surveillance. Like the supervising gaze, the novel moves toward classification by specific criminal type. The novel also follows official carceral discourse in its strategies for renouncing power; like the clinical diagnostician, Capote's narrator is both omniscient and impotent.

In Cold Blood bears the misleading subtitle "A True Account of a Multiple Murder and Its Consequences." The novel may probe the consequences of murder, but it is far more concerned with exploring the "souls" of Dick Hickock and Perry Smith perhaps chiefly by means of the flatly narrated but somehow evocative biographical anecdote. Consider the following passage, which concludes a chapter and immediately follows a discussion in which Smith and Hickock, driving through Mexico, marvel at the prospect of actually getting away with the murders they have committed: "The car was moving. A hundred feet ahead, a dog trotted along the side of the road. Dick swerved toward it. It was an old half-dead mongrel, brittle-boned and mangy, and the impact, as it met the car, was little more than what a bird might make. But Dick was satisfied. 'Boy!' he said—and it was what he always said after running down a dog, which was something he did whenever the opportunity arose. 'Boy! We sure splattered him!' " (133). This scene has little to do with the murders or their consequences, and in fact the narrator makes no direct connection, but the scene is included nonetheless, apparently as an illustration of Hickock's character. *In Cold Blood* links the murder of the Clutter family to makeshift, anecdotal biographies of the killers. In doing so the novel suggests that the meaning of the murders cannot be understood without a thorough, clinical knowledge of the people who committed them. Such knowledge permits killers who are intrinsically murderous to be separated from killers who are not.

The distinction between offender and delinquent is, as we have seen, a hallmark of the modern criminal justice system. In this sense,

109

In Cold Blood presents a sort of narrative analogue of that system. Like the novel, the prison is designed "for the formation of clinical knowledge about the convicts" (*Discipline*, 249). Descriptions of the criminal justice system offered by social historians and criminologists often echo the language Capote uses to describe *In Cold Blood*. Both are "given over to the chores of the classification of individuals and their placement and documentation" (Cousins and Hussein, 173). In both cases, "the juridical subject becomes the focal point of a classifying and objectifying mode of perception, which recruits the individual into a complex framework of justiciable characteristics and evidentiary fact" (Breuer, 236). Capote's narrative reproduces, in effect, the assessment of the criminal that takes place within the modern criminal justice system.

The concern with criminal personality type rather than criminal act is evident not only within *In Cold Blood* but also in Capote's discussions of crime in other contexts. For example, in a 1968 interview with Eric Norden, Capote explains that he is against capital punishment in the United States only because our system is so slow and arbitrary in applying it:

> If the system were clear-cut and a person was sentenced and executed within a six-month period on an even, regularized basis, then it might become a singularly effective deterrent; I think professional murderers would really think twice. By professional murderer, of course, I mean not the killer for hire or the Syndicate assassin, but the man who commits a crime with the intention of killing the man he is robbing, often in the belief that he will thus not be identified to the police by his victim. He considers murder a necessary *by-product* of his crime. [Capote, *Conversations*, 124–25]

In the present context, the most striking feature of this passage is Capote's easy assertion that there are several particular categories of killer—the assassin and the "professional" (and the unprofessional?)—which bear little resemblance to the statutory categories of homicide.

Later in the same interview, Capote elaborates on this idea as he describes his concept of the ideal way to treat killers. He advocates a system in which all homicides are treated as federal crimes, and all convicted killers are sent to a special federal prison.

110

The key to this system would be that whenever a man is convicted of first-degree homicide, he would receive no precise sentence but an indeterminate sentence of from one day to life, and the actual length of the sentence would be determined not by a parole board but by an expert psychiatric staff attached to the Federal prison. The prison itself would be as much a hospital as a jail and, unlike most of our prisons, whose so-called psychiatric staffs are merely a joke, a true effort would be made to cure the inmates. Under this system, the board might determine that the man who killed his wife in a spasm of passion would be incarcerated for only three months, since his was not a repeatable crime, while a man like Perry Smith would probably have to stay there the rest of his life. [125–26]

Under the system that Capote describes, hospitals and prisons are conflated, as are psychiatrists and prison guards, and murderers come in a variety of recognizable types.

Capote's lengthy examinations of Smith and Hickock, like his proposed psychiatric review for all first-degree murderers, result in their classification as particular criminal types. As is evident in the following excerpt from a 1966 interview with George Plimpton, Capote places himself in the position of examining psychiatrist, able to explain past crimes and predict future behavior:

Q: What do you think would have happened if Perry had faltered and not begun the killings? Do you think Dick would have done it?

A: No. There is such a thing as the ability to kill. Perry's particular psychosis had produced this ability. Dick was mostly ambitious—he could *plan* murder but not commit it. [Capote, *Conversations*, 59]

Capote's confidence in his own typing of Smith and Hickock prompts him to make this assertion even though it contradicts the findings of the official investigation. Smith's initial confession depicts Hickock as participating in the murder of Mr. Clutter and as killing the mother and daughter. According to Phillip Tompkins, who interviewed many of the participants in the case after the publication of *In Cold Blood*, most of the investigators, including county attorney Duane West and KBI agent Alvin Dewey, continued to believe that the confession was accurate.

Capote's proposed prison/hospital posits a world with various types of killer, but *In Cold Blood* focuses on one extreme end of the spec-

111

trum. The novel depicts killers so dangerous that they must never be released. The psychological profile that Capote constructs bears a striking resemblance to homicidal monomania, although the term is never used. The novel relies instead on the term "psychopath." Like the homicidal monomaniac, the murderous psychopath may appear normal and sane to the untrained eye. In both cases the derangement may go undetected until it explodes into murderous violence. A diagnosis of psychopathy requires a trained eye. Capote speaks with the confidence of a clinician when he states, in an interview, that "Perry never meant to kill the Clutters at all. He had a brain explosion" (Capote, *Conversations*, 60). Dr. Satten's report on Perry Smith, included in the novel, is likewise rooted in the paradigm of the monomaniac or psychopath:

> Such individuals can be considered to be murder-prone in the sense of either carrying a surcharge of aggressive energy or having an unstable ego defense system that periodically allows the naked and archaic expression of such energy. The murderous potential can become activated . . . when the victim-to-be is unconsciously perceived as a key figure in some past traumatic configuration. The behavior, or even the mere presence, of this figure adds a stress to the unstable balance of forces that results in a sudden extreme discharge of violence, similar to the explosion that takes place when a percussion cap ignites a charge of dynamite. [337–38]

Capote's narrator endorses Satten's diagnosis by claiming that when Smith attacked Mr. Clutter, "he was under a mental eclipse, deep inside a schizophrenic darkness" (338).

Further evidence that Capote's novel is shaped by the myth of the psychopath or monomaniac is provided by Phillip Tompkins in his article "In Cold Fact." Tompkins claims to have uncovered a number of factual errors in the book, the most serious of these being the conclusion that Perry suffered from a "brain explosion" at the time of the murders. The transcribed confessions mention nothing resembling a trancelike state or episode of altered consciousness. They seem even to rule out the possibility of a such a state. According to Smith's confession, he and Hickock discuss who will do the killing, and then Smith approaches Mr. Clutter on the pretext of tightening the ropes that bind him. Once behind Clutter, Smith produces a knife that he has been concealing and cuts Clutter's throat. Smith then hands the knife to Hickock, who repeats the act. When Clutter continues to struggle, Smith and Hickock decide to put him out of his misery by shooting him. There is evidence of planning, discussion, and a disturbingly calm demeanor, but Smith never claims that he was out of control or that he suffered from any form of seizure during the murders.

The narrative often turns directly to psychopathy in matters of diagnosis. Drawing on psychiatric testimony, particularly Satten's article about apparently unmotivated murder, Capote produces the evidence required to fit the clinical profile of the psychopath. The psychopath paradigm in the novel, however, can also be seen at work in the very structure of the narrative. The novel's diagnosis of psychopathy is confirmed by a heightened narrative vision that sees all details as potentially meaningful, all incidents as potentially anecdotal. When we read that, in preparation for their return from Mexico to the United States, Smith and Hickock ship back a carton of clothes including "two pairs of boots, one pair with soles that left a Cat's Paw print, the other pair with diamond-pattern soles" (146), we know that these details are more than documentary. That the boots are important has already been revealed by the lens of the police photographer's camera:

> As a matter of fact, one of the photographs, a close up of Mr. Clutter and the mattress box upon which he lay, had already provided a valuable surprise: footprints, the dusty trackings of shoes with diamond-patterned soles. The prints, not noticeable to the naked eye, registered on film; indeed, the delineating glare of the flashbulb had revealed their presence with superb exactness. These prints, together with another footmark found on the same cardboard cover—the bold and bloody impression of a Cat's Paw half sole—were the only "serious clues" the investigators could claim. [100]

Like the police photographer's camera, and like the trained gaze of the expert, Capote's narrator sees more than the "naked eye."

The introduction of the all-seeing narrator recreates the heightened panoptic vision used to scrutinize the prison inmate. The penitentiary posits a kind of supervision, a privileged gaze, that allows for the classification and control of each inmate. *In Cold Blood* recreates this privileged gaze by adopting a particular form of the third-person, omniscient point of view. Smith and Hickock are placed in a sort of panopticon, while the all-seeing narrator sits, himself unseen, in the observation tower.

Nowhere is the panoptic quality of the narration more evident than in the brief section following the first interviews in which Smith and Hickock are accused of the murders. Later that evening the two sit nervously in separate cells, unable to see each other or communicate. Although we know that Capote was nowhere near this scene, he has reconstructed it in such a way that the narrator is written into the observation tower, able to see not only the men but also their thoughts and feelings. Smith worries that the witness mentioned by his interrogators is an eyewitness. Hickock knows that it is Floyd Wells, the cellmate who told Hickock that the Clutter home contained a safe full of money.

In this brief chapter the narrator seems to disappear, allowing the reader direct access to the thoughts of the two prisoners. When Hickock worries about things he should have done differently, we seem to hear him speak: "Hell, if all those cowboys had to go on was some story Floyd Wells had told, then there wasn't a lot to worry about. Come right down to it, Floyd wasn't half as dangerous as Perry. Perry, if he lost his nerve and let fly, could put them both in The Corner [Kansas's Death Row]. And suddenly he saw the truth; It was *Perry* he should have silenced. On a mountain road in Mexico. Or while walking across the Mojave. Why had it never occurred to him until now? For now, now was much too late" (258). The disappearance of the narrator assures the reader that the narrative point of view is both unlimited and objective. In this particular example the narrator's disappearance demonstrates at the same time that homicide has become a way of life for Smith and Hickock.

The no-holds-barred scrutiny to which Smith and Hickock are subjected extends to all facets of their lives. A close examination of Hickock's face, for example, reveals hints about his character:

> But neither Dick's physique nor the inky gallery adorning it made as remarkable an impression as his face, which seemed composed of mismatch-

ing parts. It was as though his head had been halved like an apple, then put together a fraction off-center. Something of the kind had happened; the imperfectly aligned features were the outcome of a car collision in 1950—an accident that left his long-jawed and narrow face tilted, the left side rather lower than the right, with the results that the lips were slightly aslant, the nose askew, and his eyes not only situated at uneven levels but of uneven size, the left eye being truly serpentine, with a venomous sickly-blue squint that although it was involuntarily acquired, seemed nevertheless to warn of bitter sediment at the bottom of his nature. [43]

Through just this sort of optic phrenology, *In Cold Blood* reproduces the methods by which the criminal justice system examines and classifies its subjects. In both cases an offender is rewritten as a delinquent by means of an anecdotal biography. In both cases, too, the transformation is enabled by the construction of a heightened form of vision, one that sees things "not noticeable to the naked eye."

In order to unmask the strategies that underlie this illusion of supervision, it is necessary first to recall that psychopathy—like other variations on the homicidal monomania theme—is inseparable from narrative. Psychopaths are always defined in terms of biographical narrative. The life histories are, by definition, revisionist histories. The "trained eye" that is able to see hints of the criminal in the precriminal always reaches the scene after the fact. We view the criminal's life through his crime and thus come, almost inescapably, to see certain incidents as prophetic. In the diagnostic biography of the capital offender, the power of the murder scene is so great that it can lend a prophetic resonance to a wide variety of past events. Childhood temper tantrums foreshadow murderous rage; the absence of childhood temper tantrums reveals a psychopathic lack of affect. When the incident happened, it lacked significance. Later, when it was seen "properly," in the light of eventual violence, it became anecdote.

In Cold Blood promotes such resonance through suggestive epigrams, titles, and subtitles and by juxtaposing scenes of people we know are about to be killed with scenes of people we know are their killers. The style of the narrative may be flat and objective, but no scene can be "merely" documentary when it is preceded by a subtitle like "The Last to See Them Alive." By the time readers catch their first glimpse of Perry Smith, they may find that they too are acquiring

115

a trained eye: "Like Mr. Clutter, the young man breakfasting in a cafe called the 'Little Jewel' never drank coffee. He preferred root beer. Three aspirin, cold root beer, and a chain of Pall Mall cigarettes—that was his notion of a proper 'chow down.' Sipping and smoking, he studied a map spread on the counter before him—a Phillips 66 map of Mexico—but it was difficult to concentrate, for he was expecting a friend, and the friend was late" (24). This scene reverberates with prophetic meaning because of the subtitle and other textual indications that tranquillity is about to erupt into violence. The immediately preceding sentence, for example, depicts Herb Clutter with awful prescience: "Touching the brim of his cap, he headed for home and the day's work, unaware that it would be his last" (24). Mr. Clutter may be unaware, but the all-seeing narrator is not. The same privileged gaze that scrutinizes Smith and Hickock in their cells can look into the past, in effect bringing history under surveillance.

The narrative also relies on another strategy for reproducing the sort of supervision posited by the criminal justice system and by diagnostic biography: the inclusion of testimony from witnesses and experts. Just as a trial transcript assembles testimony from a wide range of witnesses and experts, the novel incorporates various documents relating to the case. Capote quotes at length from the statements of various criminologists, criminal psychiatrists, and law enforcement officials. He also reproduces autobiographical confessions by Smith and Hickock as well as biographical testimony about the two from their surviving parents. The narrative establishes and validates through expert testimony and documentation a profile of a specific criminal type and then proceeds to wed the facts of the Clutter "case" to that profile.

Among the external documents included are brief autobiographies written by each of the defendants. Dr. Jones requests these written statements and uses them, along with interviews lasting about two hours, as the basis for the psychological evaluations that are excluded from the trial but included in the novel. Near the beginning of Smith's statement, he recalls a fight with his brother:

The next thing I can recall is living in Fort Bragg, Calif. My brother had been presented a B.B. gun. He had shot a hummingbird, and after he had shot it he was sorry. I asked him to let me shoot the B.B. gun. He pushed me away, telling me I was too small. It made me so mad I started to cry. After I finished crying, my anger mounted again, and during the evening when the B.B. gun was behind the chair my brother was sitting in, I grabbed it & held it to my brother's ear & hollered BANG! My father (or mother) beat me and made me apologize. [308]

It is difficult not to read this incident as prefiguring the later murders. The dispute with his brother recalls Smith's later altercation with brother-figure Hickock, which ended when Smith took a shotgun from Hickock and pointed it at four (or was it two?) other heads. Our sense of the line between the episodes is heightened by the fact that Smith chose to include the otherwise unremarkable memory from childhood early in his statement. It is the second story recounted in a brief autobiography that begins with the story of Smith's birth.

There are, however, some problems with reading the incident as particularly prophetic. For example, we cannot be sure what went on between Smith and Hickock in the Clutter house or even who did the killing. Even more of a problem is that the presence of ellipses in the statement indicates that it has been edited: what has been omitted? Furthermore, we have no way of knowing what sort of primacy Smith assigned to the incident. How many stories were omitted before one could be found with such sinister resonance? Who made the decision? Also, is it possible that Smith's experience with prison psychiatrists "trained" him to produce evocative anecdotes like these?

A statement that, after all, Capote did not even write thus emerges as an instrument of manipulation carefully honed for effect. Like the "trained eye" of the diagnostician, Capote's narrator is able to look into the past and identify precriminal behavior. In the sense that the narrator both exercises and renounces power by including this fragment, the BB gun story is typical of the way that both the novel and the criminal justice system make useful anecdotes from "useless" incidents.

A shadowy figure haunts the final pages of *In Cold Blood*: a journalist who is mentioned twice as he interviews Dick Hickock on Death Row. It is revealed that this journalist, who corresponds with Hickock and visits him regularly, is "equally well acquainted with [Perry] Smith"

(371, 375). The journalist is not mentioned again, and we are left to wonder about his identity and role in the story. This mysterious figure is probably Capote, but why would he choose to disguise himself in this manner?

There are no direct references to Capote in the narrative. Capote claimed that this anonymity was a central element of his experiment in the "nonfiction novel": "The real demarcation between my book and anything that has gone before is that it contains a technical innovation that gives it both the reality and the atmosphere of a novel; and that device is that I never once appear in the book. Never" (Capote, *Conversations*, 120). Although Capote claims that the erasure of the "I" from the text is largely a "technical innovation" to avoid the intrusiveness of the first person, I suggest that this decision should be seen as part of a larger renunciation of power that is—paradoxically—best understood as a strategy for masking the exercise of power.

The simultaneous exercise and denial of power characterize diagnostic biography as it functions within the criminal justice system. The rewriting of an offender as a delinquent or psychopath, for example, is an act of power in which a criminal act is determined to be evidence of a criminal personality type in one offender but not another. This distinction may justify the maximum punishment in the former case and the minimum in the latter, but it is disguised as discovery or diagnosis. Once an offender is discovered to be a delinquent or a psychopath, the criminal justice system must respond, but even then disciplinary power appears to be exercised reluctantly and after the fact. Because delinquency is dangerous, the criminal justice system must step in and protect the public interest by imprisoning, and possibly executing, anyone discovered to be a delinquent. Also, because the models for delinquency and psychopathy identify visible symptoms that begin to appear during childhood (at least to properly trained eyes), diagnostic biography establishes that the criminal justice system plays no role in the production of criminality.

If we are to trace the workings of power in carceral narratives, then, we must come to terms with power's dissembling strategies. Disciplinary power manifests itself in discourse not as admonition or command but as diagnosis. For every exercise of power there is an accompanying disavowal. *In Cold Blood* reproduces strategies for the simultaneous exercise and denial of power that can also be seen at work in much carceral discourse. The novel characterizes itself as merely observing and recording what is, after all, a true story and thus works to deny that it has transformed or distorted this story in any way. This renunciation of power appears on several different levels of the narrative.

One way for a writer to renounce power is to lay a claim to realism. Capote goes further. His narrative, he declares, is not only realistic but also completely and utterly true, a nonfiction novel. Given the nature of the project, any departure from fact is unacceptable. Capote once stated that "one doesn't spend almost six years on a book, the point of which is factual accuracy, and then give way to minor distortions" (Capote, *Conversations*, 62). He goes so far as to describe himself as a "literary photographer" and also states that he spent two hours a day, for eighteen months, training himself to be a human tape-recorder (Capote, *Conversations*, 48, 54).

The narrative supports the illusion of complete objectivity by recording numerous details that later prove to have no connection to the crime. Like the camera and the tape-recorder, the narrative thus seems to record without interpreting or editing. We are told, for example, that in the days before the murders, Nancy Clutter smells cigarette smoke in the house, an oddity in a home where smoking was forbidden. On the last day of his life, Mr. Clutter encounters a group of strangers armed with shotguns and gives them permission to hunt on his land. Hours before his death, Mr. Clutter signed a new life insurance policy. These incidents will prove unrelated to the murders. Their inclusion establishes that the narrator sees with a undiscriminating eye and leads us to believe that we are not being manipulated.

The novel's reliance on external documentation and expert testimony, as previously noted, reinforces the illusion of documentary realism. Long passages are quoted verbatim from confessions, letters, psychiatric evaluations, and transcriptions of court proceedings, thus providing further evidence that the novel is reporting rather than interpreting or creating. Capote also labors to support these claims of documentary realism in interviews, as when he tells George Plimpton that his "files would almost fill a whole small room, right up to the ceiling. All my research. Hundreds of letters. Newspaper clippings. Court Records" (Capote, *Conversations*, 66).

Perhaps the primary strategy for renouncing power can be discovered through an exploration of Capote's theory of the nonfiction novel, which posits an absolute separation of art and power. Capote even denies that the nonfiction novel has anything to do with crime: "In a way, I guess it was unfortunate that I selected a crime for my first big experiment in the genre [nonfiction novel], because that made it easier for them to . . . think of it as a true crime story. But a nonfiction novel can be about *anything*—from crime to butterfly collecting" (Capote, *Conversations*, 122). Capote also claims that his work on the Clutter case grew not out of an interest in crime but out of a desire to wed the techniques of journalism to those of fiction: "the motivating factor in my choice of material—that is, choosing to write a true account of an actual murder case—was altogether literary" (Capote, *Conversations*, 47). Even in this choice of subject matter Capote seems at pains to deny any hint of exercising power, claiming that he "*didn't* select this Kansas farmer and his family; in a very real sense, they selected me" (Capote, *Conversations*, 122).

By emphasizing that his motives were "altogether literary," Capote posits a disjunction between style and subject matter, between the workings of the criminal justice system and the workings of the artist. The nonfiction novelist, like the diagnostician, is a slave to fact and makes decisions only concerning the manner of presentation. According to Capote, too, the nonfiction novelist must remain completely removed from political or ideological motivations. Capote claims to have told Perry Smith that the book "didn't have anything to do with changing the reader's opinion about anything, nor did I have any moral reasons worthy of calling them such—it was just that I had a strictly aesthetic theory about creating a book which could result in a work of art" (Nichols, 39).

All of these strategies for renouncing power—asserting factual accuracy, providing supporting documents, claiming aesthetic disinterest and egoless objectivity—are evident in carceral discourse in general and especially in diagnostic biography. They work to mask the physical mechanism of power, which, both in Capote's novel and the criminal justice system, is largely embodied in the prison and in diagnostic biography. Diagnostic biography renders the prison invisible. For example, by locating evidence of delinquency in the subject's childhood, the narrative indicates that the criminal justice system plays no role in the production of delinquency. When Capote makes the curious decision virtually to ignore the years his subjects have spent behind bars, to ignore the institution in which the murder plan was hatched, in which all of Capote's interviews with the killers took place, and which played such a profound role in the lives of his subjects, he does the same thing.

The decision to erase the author, to adopt a third-person, omniscient point of view, allows us to read the novel without thinking about the fact that Capote never saw his subjects outside police custody and that he never spoke to them outside prison. The physical fact of their incarceration seems to have been significant only as an inconvenience to Capote's project. Incarceration was fundamental to the project, however, and offered Capote certain advantages with respect to his subjects. "I could always tell when Dick or Perry wasn't telling the truth. During the first few months or so of interviewing them, they weren't allowed to speak to each other. They were in separate cells. So I would keep crossing their stories, and what correlated, what checked out identically, was the truth" (Capote, *Conversations*, 57–58).

In Cold Blood reveals little trace of the "I" of this statement or of the process by which Smith and Hickock's stories were collected and cross-checked. All that survives in the final text is the sense of absolute certitude, of complete knowledge of a subject. Erasing the "I" from the text may appear to diminish the influence of the author, but instead it allows the substitution of an objective, infallible, panoptic eye for the subjective, fallible, normally-sighted "I" of the writer. The prison disappears, and a sort of leveling effect is achieved as each incident recounted in the narrative becomes equally true. The different layers of distortion, fabrication, coercion, folklore, and twenty-twenty hindsight are hidden beneath the surface. Every episode of the narrative takes on a uniform, visual verisimilitude.

This dark area of the narrative, which allows the mechanisms of power to remain hidden, apparently distinguishes mainstream nonfiction from Capote's "nonfiction novel." Capote's paradigm is meant for a hybrid form that uses novelistic techniques in writing nonfiction narrative. The awkward term "nonfiction novel" highlights a contradiction: if the narrative is factually accurate, and thus nonfiction, why is the word "novel" necessary? The inadequacy of the term "nonfiction" as a description suggests that the story does something other than recount fact. Capote addresses this issue by introducing an intriguing metaphor:

> But what I wanted to do was bring to journalism the technique of fiction, which moves both horizontally and vertically at the same time: horizontally on the narrative side and vertically by entering inside its characters. . . . Now, in my effort to give journalism this vertical interior movement— and that was the whole purpose of my experiment—I had to remove the narrator entirely. I had to make the book flow uninterruptedly from beginning to end, just like a novel, and thus the narrator never enters the picture and there is no interpretation of people and events. . . . except for the selection of detail, I am totally absent from the development of the book, and the people are re-created as they are in life. [120]

The introduction of this vertical, novelistic axis, which moves "inside" characters and events while avoiding interpretation, creates some obvious problems; to represent the "inside" of character or plot *is* to interpret. Capote's method masks the agency of power while retaining the effects of that power. An illusion of objectivity is maintained because the author avoids stating his interpretation outright, but the narrative is structured in such a way that the reader's interpretation is managed, shaped, and controlled.

The problems inherent in an uncritical acceptance of the narrative's objectivity become apparent in passages like the following, from Kenneth T. Reed:

> It is significant that Capote at no time renders a judgment about the criminals. His determined disinterest is maintained for at least two reasons: it is important for the reader to draw his own conclusions about the philosophical-sociological-psychological circumstances of the mass murder, and Capote was determined not to interfere with the reader's judgmental process. . . . Capote is primarily concerned with motivations and circumstances that form an engrossing but inscrutable web of factors that rendered Smith and Hickock moral invalids, psychopathic criminals. It be-

122

comes evident that questions of condemnation and sympathy toward the criminals have no real bearing from an objective standpoint. [107]

Reed is confident that his assessment of Smith and Hickock as "psychopathic criminals" and "moral invalids" is his own, that it does not originate in the novel. The novel presents only raw fact, he seems to be saying, and a discerning reader like Reed knows a psychopath when he sees one.

By adopting these dissembling strategies, then, the novel, like much penal discourse, masks the exercise of power. But what does this power accomplish, and what forms does it take? In a broad sense, disciplinary power can be said to work toward exclusion and normalization. A particular segment of the population is excluded from society—through incarceration or execution—and carceral discourse produces the diagnostic biographies that justify this exclusion. These narratives explain the treatment of criminals for the benefit of the remaining, law-abiding segment of the population, but also reinforce a vision of society in which the idealized domestic hearth serves as norm. By producing, classifying, and managing various forms of criminality, the criminal justice system defines the normal and the abnormal while creating an atmosphere of danger that demands a careful distinction between the two.

Foucault argues that two of the main "instruments" of disciplinary power are hierarchical observation and normalizing judgment (*Discipline*, 170). These categories provide a useful way of approaching the subject of power in *In Cold Blood*. The narrator's vision, like the privileged gaze of surveillance, sees its subjects while remaining unseen. In a sense, the narrator subsumes the investigating detective, the examining psychiatrist, the sentencing judge, and the guard in the observation tower. From this lofty position, the narrator may even see more than these intermediary agents could, as when Agent Dewey doggedly pursues leads that we know are false.

The hierarchical nature of the relationship between narrator and subject in the novel is further illustrated by the narrator's role as confessor to Smith and Hickock. Capote takes on this position of authority, extracting confessions from Smith and Hickock and embedding those confessions in a narrative that judges, qualifies, and evaluates them. Like the police interrogators when they take official confessions, Capote verifies the accuracy of confessions by cross-checking them against one another and against other external sources. He judges Smith's official confession, in which Smith claims that Hickock killed the two women, to be false, even though it was accepted by the court and many of the chief investigators on the case. Capote rejects this confession in favor of one that credits Smith with all four murders. In doing so once again he affirms the narrator's position atop the hierarchy of observation.

Capote may also have departed from the facts in his depiction of Smith as repentant and apologetic. Capote reports that Smith cried in his cell after the trial, that he held the hand of Mrs. Meier (the wife of the undersheriff) and sobbed, "I'm embraced by shame" (Tompkins, 345). Capote also writes that Smith apologized for his crimes just before mounting the scaffold. Tompkins interviewed Mrs. Meier and several people who witnessed the executions. He claims that all disputed Capote's version. Mrs. Meier denied that she ever heard Smith cry or claim to be ashamed and, vehemently, that she ever held his hand. Tompkins also spoke with witnesses at the execution who were confident that Smith did not apologize.

The portrait of a repentant Smith may not fit the facts, but it does seem curiously consistent with the model for confession in a disciplinary hierarchy. In such a system, confession has a twofold purpose: it serves both to reveal the truth and to transform the confessor. The confession is a "ritual in which the expression alone, independently of its external consequences, produces intrinsic modification in the person who articulates it: it exonerates, redeems, and purifies" (Foucault, *History*, 62). Such a model may help explain why Capote sees remorse in Smith when others do not. Capote's role as confessor would be incomplete without Smith's repentance.

In Cold Blood exercises normalizing judgment largely in its manipulation of images of the domestic hearth. The idealized domesticity of the Clutter family contrasts especially starkly in the novel with the nomadic criminality of Smith and Hickock. Capote seems at pains to present Herb Clutter as the ideal head of a perfect family. He is "the master of River Valley Farm" (15). Although he is short and wears glasses, he is a "man's man" (16). Not the town's richest citizen, he is nonetheless its most prominent. He married "the person he had wished to marry" (16), and his daughter is the "town darling" (17). He is kind but firm with his children: "his laws were laws" (18). Through good sense and years of hard work, Clutter has come to embody the American dream of the self-made man running a successful family farm. Against this portrait of productivity and ingenuity the novel places Perry Smith, an aimless ex-convict without money or prospects, a drifter capable of killing without remorse and without a second thought.

In an interview with Eric Norden, Capote claims that Clutter and Smith embody the extremes of American life:

> The Clutter family and Smith and Hickock do represent the opposite poles in American society; if you ask me who best represents the *real* America, I have to say a very modified and much more soiled and complicated version of the Clutter family. But Perry Smith . . . does represent a very real side of American life; he is typical of the conscienceless yet perversely sensitive violence that runs through such phenomena as the motorcycle gangs and the drifting herds of brutalized children wandering across the country. [Capote, *Conversations*, 133–34]

One of the interesting things about this passage is that it posits at least a potential disjunction between criminality and domesticity; were it not for the predatory nature of these nomadic psychopaths, the idealized domestic hearth would remain intact and would never be soiled by the criminal.

The disjunction between criminality and domesticity proves, however, to be quite problematic. In the novel, the two are inseparable opposing poles of American society. The initial appearance of disjunction dissolves under scrutiny to reveal interdependence and entanglement. As *In Cold Blood* locates the source of criminality outside the criminal justice system, it tends to locate it within the family. More specifically, criminality reflects a family's failure to measure up to the domestic ideal. The murders are the manifestation of the abuse Smith suffered at the hands of a drunken mother and the final resolution of his love-hate relationship with his shiftless father. When the narrative includes its edited version of Smith's autobiography, the only story that precedes the BB gun anecdote is one in which a young

Smith watches in horror as his father beats his mother because she was drinking and "entertaining" a group of sailors (308). This is Smith's "primal" scene, and it leads directly to the first sign of his murderous nature.

Criminality and the family are also linked in the future. The novel envisions the idealized domestic hearth as a site ripe for violence. Capote in his description of the relationship between Clutter and Smith insists that the murders were fated: "All this had to happen; there was a quality of inevitability about it. Given what Perry was, and what the Clutters represented, the only possible outcome of their convergence was death" (Capote, *Conversations*, 134).

It is not surprising that the novel depicts the destruction of the Clutter family as foreordained; what is surprising is that domesticity linked with violence can be seen whenever an idealized family setting is depicted. The novel describes the home of Smith's only surviving sister, for example, in terms that emphasize cheerful, all-American domesticity. The Johnson family (Capote protects the family with this appropriate pseudonym) lives in "a middle-class, middle-income real estate development" near San Francisco, in a "conventional suburban ranch house, pleasant and commonplace." Mrs. Johnson is "in love with" the house and especially its backyard: "And she was proud of the small back garden; her husband—by profession an insurance salesman, by inclination a carpenter—had built around it a white picket fence, and inside it a house for the family dog, and a sandbox and swings for the children. At the moment, all four—dog, two little boys, and a girl—were playing there under a mild sky" (205–6). Despite this idyllic setting, Mrs. Johnson is haunted by fears of violence, both at the hands of her brother Perry and in more impersonal forms. She is tormented by thoughts that she will "go mad, or contract an incurable illness, or in a fire lose all she valued—home, husband, children." At the end of the brief chapter describing Mrs. Johnson, she is troubled by her fears, hiding behind doors locked against "the dead as well as the living" (213–14).

The novel's tendency to locate the source of violent criminality in failed family units may also explain why Capote rejects the theory that Smith and Hickock were both murderers. Smith's family life was sordid enough to produce a psychopathic killer, but Hickock's childhood offers no such colorful images of squalor or abuse. Capote may have rejected the idea that Hickock could also be a murderer on the ground that his parents seemed relatively normal.

Such links between criminal violence and domestic bliss are perhaps best understood in terms of what Foucault dismisses as the "repressive hypothesis" of power. Repressive theories envision disciplinary power and criminality as adversaries, with power struggling to eliminate the criminals, namely those who resist power. Crime may persist, even flourish, but only because of failures in the execution of the penal plan, not because of flaws in the plan itself. As an alternative to repressive theories of power, Foucault argues that we see power instead as producing and using delinquency. In terms of handling offenders, delinquency allows for exclusion, for the separation of a certain segment of the population. The criminal justice system "is not intended to eliminate offences, but rather to distinguish them, to distribute them, to use them . . . to assimilate the transgression of the laws in a general tactics of subjection" (*Discipline*, 272).

The presence of delinquency can also be used, however, to exert a normalizing influence on the remaining segment of society. As has been illustrated, biographical portraits of delinquents tend to link horrific crimes to a wide array of minor illegalities and legal nonconformity. This linkage tends to make all nonconformity seem dangerous. By locating the source of criminality in domestic failures, these biographies increase the pressure on parents to "discipline" their children. Carceral narratives promote an image of normalcy under siege, depicting idealized domestic settings as the favored targets of murderous young psychopaths. Delinquents come to represent an eminent public danger that necessitates, even requires, a police presence.

Disciplinary power works, then, largely by creating a sense of danger. *In Cold Blood* participates in and reproduces that manufacturing of danger. Perry Smith must be presented not as a small-time hood who, one night, under extraordinary circumstances, participates in a brutal mass murder but instead as a compulsive killer, a man particularly inflamed by the sight of a happy family and eager to murder again. Capote often described Smith using such terms:

127

Perry Smith was a serious psychopath and to some degree paranoid, with the kind of mind that is able to kill without passion and without remorse, just as you or I would swat a fly. I've known several Perry types, and human life means nothing to them; it's as if they have a talent for destruction, the kind of death-dealing ability hired killers have. . . . They can cut a man's throat from ear to ear and walk away and go to a movie and never think about what they've just done, because they place no value whatever on human life. [Capote, *Conversations*, 128–29]

This assessment of Smith is inconsistent not only with other accounts of the case but also with the the novel itself. More than once we are told that Smith worries about his role in the murders, thinking that "there's got to be something wrong with somebody who'd do a thing like that." Smith worries this point so incessantly that Hickock, who would rather forget the incident, is irritated almost to the point of violence: "Christ Jesus, what damn good did it do, always dragging the goddamn thing up" (128–29).

In addition to this evidence of Smith's anguish and self-doubt, the novel also establishes that Smith and Hickock were never involved in any other killings. Perry may have been able to cut a man's throat as easily and thoughtlessly as he would swat a fly, but he never did so. Even so, Capote is able to assert that a "pattern of homicide had become so ingrained in them that it was inevitable they would have killed again had they remained free" (Capote, *Conversations*, 130). To support this statement, Capote can only cite plans of murder that never materialize, and Smith's admittedly fabricated story about killing a man years before the Clutter murders. Capote's assertions may not represent the facts of the case, but they do foster an aura of danger around Smith and Hickock, an aura that works both to exclude the pair from the human race and to justify the "work" of penal power.

Capote's depictions of cold-blooded killers often owe more to popular images of the psychopath than to the details of a particular case, perhaps because Capote wanted to stress the danger they represented. In describing one of the other inmates housed with Smith and Hickock on Death Row, for example, Capote seems to draw on the words of Flannery O'Connor's Misfit, from the story "A Good Man Is Hard to Find." James Douglas Latham is quoted as saying,

"It's a rotten world. . . . There's no answer to it but meanness. That's all anybody understands—meanness. Burn down the man's barn—he'll understand that. Poison his dog. Kill him" (362). O'Connor's Misfit makes another appearance as Hickock tells his story to the mysterious journalist:

> When that boy read a book it stayed read. Course he didn't know a dumb-darn thing about life. Me, I'm an ignoramus except when it comes to what I know about life. I've walked along a lot of mean streets. I've seen a white man flogged. I've watched babies born. I've seen a girl, and her no more than fourteen, take on three guys at the same time and give them all their money's worth. Fell off a ship once five miles out to sea. Swam five miles with my life passing before me every stroke. Once I shook hands with President Truman in the lobby of the Hotel Muehlebach. Harry S. Truman. [373]

Capote's choice of the Misfit as model psychopath is especially noteworthy, because O'Connor's story also depicts a man, recently out of prison, who murders an entire family in cold blood.[2]

By forging these links between criminality and domesticity, and by creating the image of a family home that is besieged by inhuman monsters, the novel can be said to do for the reader what the Clutter murders do for the town of Holcomb. The once innocent, peaceful town is transformed. People begin locking their doors and eyeing one another suspiciously. Even after Smith and Hickock are arrested and have made their confessions, many residents of the town remain on guard: "a sizable faction refused to accept the fact that two unknown men, two thieving strangers, were solely responsible" (262). For these citizens, Smith and Hickock must have been hired killers working for someone who knew the Clutters, probably someone from Holcomb. The atmosphere of eminent danger creates the need for increased police surveillance and heightened security measures. Even Detective Alvin Dewey and his wife put aside their long-held dream of owning a farmhouse outside of town, too fearful to live in such isolation (382).

In Cold Blood, like many narratives of delinquency and incarcera-

---

[2]For the apparent sources of the two quoted passages, see *Three by Flannery O'Connor* (140, 142).

tion, is generally considered sympathetic to its subjects. Capote freely admitted that he came to think of Smith and Hickock as his close friends, and many critics have noted that Capote especially identified with Smith. It has also been pointed out that the title seems to describe the executions that end the novel more aptly than the murders that begin it. Capote's inclusion of psychological profiles of the subjects that the court chose to exclude adds to our sense that the novel is deliberately critical of the judicial system and particularly of the system's stance on questions of mental illness.

These images of sympathy and criticism, however, fail under careful scrutiny. Although Capote may regard Smith and Hickock as friends, he considers them too dangerous ever to be released from prison. His novel may include the excluded psychological testimony, but this testimony makes the pair seem more dangerous by portraying them as murderous time bombs virtually guaranteed to explode and kill again. Capote's sympathy resembles the pastoral "care" that characterizes disciplinary power. His criticism of the judicial system, if acted upon, would only extend and strengthen that system. Because carceral power manages and even produces the forces that would resist it, *In Cold Blood* can only reproduce the incarceration of its subjects.

I have become a stranger to my needs and desires. And without meaning to sound conceited or to brag, I can honestly say I cannot imagine anyone with more moral stamina, more psychological endurance and more will power than I myself have. I have measured these things and I know.

You can't know how sad I feel when I realize the source of, and the nature of, the *involuntary* pride and exhilaration all convicts feel when they are chained up hand and foot as though they were vicious lions, dangerous animals. They make killers out of pussycats like that.
—Jack Henry Abbott, *In the Belly of the Beast*

S I X

Norman Mailer's *The Executioner's Song:* Strategies of Defiance

The novels examined so far have stopped short of depicting the act of execution. Norris avoids the subject altogether. Patrick Collins, the original for McTeague, was hanged, but McTeague evades the authorities and is last seen awaiting death in the desert. Dreiser documents Clyde Griffiths's path toward the electric chair in exhaustive detail for more than eight hundred pages but turns away discreetly as Clyde crosses the threshold into the execution chamber. Wright wrote a scene describing Bigger's death but then decided not to include it. Like *An American Tragedy, Native Son* leaves its protagonist just before the execution is carried out. Capote describes the hangings of Perry Smith and Dick Hickock but through the eyes of observers reluctant to watch the proceedings. The actual executions are reduced to a few sentences, most of which describe sounds and glimpses of dangling feet.

Norman Mailer exhibits no such squeamishness about the execution of Gary Gilmore. Mailer's obsession with detail seems to increase as the narrative approaches the moment of death. The account of Gilmore's final forty-eight hours and the disposal of his body, at 157 pages, is as long as a good-sized novel. More than ten pages are devoted to the few minutes that Gilmore spends strapped in the execution chair. The narrative lingers over the shooting and the thirty seconds or so required for Gilmore's death and then follows the body into the autopsy room. In this excruciating scene, readers watch while a man whose life they have followed for over a thousand pages is sliced into bits. The doctor in charge "skinned Gilmore right up over his shoulders like taking a shirt half off, and with a saw cut right up the breastbone to the throat, and removed the breastplate and set it in a big, open sink with running water" (1009–10).

> After this, it got really gruesome. Jerry had to admit it. They started removing different parts of Gilmore's body. Took his plumbing out, stomach, entrails and everything, then cut little pieces out of each organ. One guy was up at the head just working away. Next thing you knew, he had Gilmore's tongue in his hand. "Why take that?" asked Jerry Scott. He didn't know whether his questions bothered the doctors or not, but since he had to witness, he thought he might as well find out what was going on. The dissectionist answered, "We're going to take a sample of it." Put the tongue down on the slab, cut it in half and sliced out a piece. Put it in a bottle of solution. [1010]

Why should *The Executioner's Song* differ in this way from the more circumspect execution novels that I considered earlier in this book? Is Mailer sensationalizing his material, or is he attempting merely to be more thorough than his predecessors in recording the facts? The public representation of an execution, especially behind closed doors, is a politically loaded act. By narrating Gilmore's execution, Mailer unveils for the public a ceremony that, despite international media scrutiny, is performed behind closed doors. The execution occurs on prison grounds, in a building shielded from the eyes of the public and the hundreds of journalists sent to cover the story. Larry Schiller, whose report on the execution provides the basis for most of Mailer's account, is allowed to witness only because he is on the small list of friends and family members whom Gilmore is permitted to invite. Prison authorities forbid the use of any recording devices, but Schiller is able to sneak in a small tape-recorder, and he also takes extensive notes during the proceedings. From its inception, then, Mailer's account of the execution is grounded in defiance of carceral authority.

The representation of execution is a politically loaded act in a wider sense too. As Foucault has argued, spectacular executions may consolidate the power of the state or monarch through public demonstration, but they also run the risk of inciting rebellion. *Discipline and Punish* opens with a horrific account of the 1757 torture and execution of Damiens the regicide. The proceedings are recounted in the detached, officious style of the civil servant or amateur naturalist (most of the material is quoted from contemporary accounts), and the ritual is badly botched. The sulfur used to scorch the offending hand burns poorly and seems to disappoint those in charge. The pincers designed to tear the flesh from breast, arms, thighs, and calves also fail to fulfill expectations; they are difficult even for the sturdy executioner to operate and produce wounds scarcely larger than a "six pound crown piece" (4). The attempt to rip Damiens limb from limb is likewise problematic. The four horses prove unequal to the task, and Damiens is successfully quartered only after the executioner cuts through his thighs and adds two more horses to the team.

Because the ceremony does not live up to the authoritative language of the proclamation that demanded it, the executioners risk appearing sadistic and incompetent rather than powerful and magisterial. The bungling of the execution shows that such spectacles can turn "the legal violence of the executioner into shame" (9). This shamefulness is further highlighted by the exemplary behavior of the condemned man, who blesses his executioners and implores them not to curse even as they harness the fifth and sixth horses.

When executions are moved behind closed doors, the meaning of capital punishment in public discourse changes. As execution becomes less visible, it comes increasingly to be known secondhand, through representation in journalistic narrative and other forms of public discourse. The move indoors may be explained and justified in the name of common decency, but it also means that public perceptions of capital punishment are increasingly grounded in the abstract

133

and in the potentially mythic. By violating the secrecy of the execution chamber, Mailer at least rhetorically reinstates the public scaffold. The act of execution leaves its protected quarters behind prison walls—where Dreiser, for example, is content to leave it—and reenters the world of the concrete, the public, and the visible.

Rendered in vivid, exact terms, Gilmore's execution is fully capable of provoking outrage. Throughout the execution scene, Mailer's narrator tells us how the physical details of setting and ceremony violate the expectations of the observers. Schiller is shocked to see that the execution chair is "no more than a little old office chair" backed by a hastily constructed bullet stop of sandbags and a filthy mattress (980). One observer is "incensed" to see Utah's director of corrections "dancing around greeting people, practically gallivanting with his big white cowboy hat, looking like a Texas bureaucrat" (981). Another complains that Sam Smith, the prison warden, has admitted any "cop or bureaucrat with a little pull" and is reminded of a friend's assertion that Smith is "totally incompetent" (980).

Immediately after Gilmore has been declared dead, the doctor, the warden, and the chaplain unstrap the body from its chair and begin to examine the wounds. To Ron Stanger, Gilmore's attorney, this procedure seems to be yet another violation of decorum: "Stanger was furious. The moment Gilmore was shot, everybody should have been walked out, and not served for a party to all this. Even as Sam was examining the body, Gary fell over into Meersman's hands. The padre had to hold the head while Sam went fishing all over Gilmore's back to locate the exit wounds. Blood started coming onto Meersman's hands, and dripped through his fingers, and Vern began to weep" (987–88).

As in the execution of Damiens, the behavior of the condemned man in the moments before death is restrained and dignified enough to highlight the indignity of the subsequent proceedings. Several observers comment on Gilmore's strength and control, marveling at his ability to joke and carry on conversations while being strapped into the execution chair. One witness "could not believe the calm he saw in that man. Gilmore was so strong in his desire to die right, that he didn't clench his fist as the count began" (985–86).

Mailer's willingness to violate the privacy of the execution scene is but one of a number of ways in which *The Executioner's Song* attempts to resist or undermine the dominant discourse. In previous chapters, I showed that the myth of the psychopath or born criminal enables the extension of penal power; the myth provides blueprints for the biographies that rewrite particular criminal offenders as criminal personality types. It might also be argued, however, that myth can work in the opposite direction. If the myth of the psychopath can function to subordinate certain individuals to systemic power, is it not possible that countermyths allow certain individuals to triumph over that power?

Such countermyths appear in the folklore, literature, and culture of prisoners. Careful examination reveals that Mailer has exploited these sources. Like Gilmore, Mailer draws on popular images of the hardened convict, or criminal "hardman," in fashioning a strategy of resistance. Gilmore defies authority, both before and after his arrest, by manifesting a cold-blooded, unpredictable, and violent persona. At every opportunity he flaunts his contempt for the police, the prison staff, and the judicial system. He admits to his crimes but refuses to apologize for them or to elaborate on his motivations. Instead of appealing his sentence, he accepts it and seems to welcome death. In short, he plays to the hilt the role of hardened convict—despised and feared by prison authorities, admired and feared by fellow inmates. He styles himself a brutal, emotionally detached stoic, a man acting in accordance with a personal agenda both separate from and superior to society's laws.

Mailer's strategy of resistance is likewise entangled with the myths of the hardened convict and the cold-blooded killer. His interest in such figures predates his involvement with Gilmore's story by at least two decades. In "The White Negro: Superficial Reflections on the Hipster" (1957), Mailer proposes that criminal transgression and psychopathy are effective strategies for resisting society's efforts to police the normal and to force each citizen toward conformity. For Mailer's white Negro or hipster, violent crime becomes a romantic act of self-destruction and re-creation, a way of forming "a new nervous system" (318). The similarities between Gilmore as Mailer portrays him and his psychopathic white Negro do not mean, however, that Mailer distorts Gilmore's character to fit a preconceived model. There is

135

ample evidence that Gilmore actively represented himself as a hardened convict and a cold-blooded killer. If he resembles Mailer's hipster, it must be remembered that Mailer and Gilmore drew on the same outlaw strand of popular culture.

In apparent opposition to the dominant discourse described in preceding chapters, then, there is a tradition of resistant discourse by and about career criminals. *The Executioner's Song* can be seen to reproduce the strategies of that resistant tradition in a number of ways. For example, the novel allows Gilmore to voice a critique of the prison system and uses subtle indicators to affirm that critique. The novel also follows Gilmore's lead in refusing to accept the deterministic readings of his life set forth by official diagnostic biography. Like Gilmore, the narrator of *The Executioner's Song* seems attuned to the strategic value of silence; both freely admit the "facts" of the case but refrain from drawing connections, reaching conclusions, or diagnosing. Finally, the novel cooperates with Gilmore in forcing the executioners to do their work on the mass-media equivalent of the public scaffold.

In the summer of 1976, when thirty-five-year-old Gary Mark Gilmore was released on parole from the federal penitentiary in Marion, Illinois, the nation had gone nine years without an execution. In June of 1967 Colorado executed Luis Monge, a convicted murderer who demanded that his death sentence be carried out; after that, executions ceased altogether. Five years later the Supreme Court, in *Furman v. Georgia*, struck down all existing death penalty statutes while simultaneously ruling that capital punishment was not inherently unconstitutional. In the ensuing years, thirty-five states drafted new death penalty legislation designed to meet the criteria for lawful executions as described in the *Furman v. Georgia* decision.

Few could have foreseen that Gilmore would become the first person executed under the new laws. When he was paroled into the care of his aunt and uncle in Provo, Utah, it was clear that the newly drafted statutes would soon be tested. At the time, there were over four hundred people under sentence of death around the country, and many of these inmates were nearing the end of the appeals process. It would have seemed unlikely, if not impossible, for someone outside prison to move to the head of this line. Furthermore,

Gilmore's fight for parole had succeeded because he had in recent years shown signs of rehabilitation. It was true that he had been incarcerated for virtually all of his adult life, but his crimes had typically been petty ones. There was no evidence that his violence would ever turn murderous.

The Executioner's Song devotes most of its attention to the period between Gilmore's parole and his execution. Initially, he moves in with his aunt and uncle, Ida and Vern Damico. He works briefly in his uncle's shoe repair shop, but after an embarrassing fight with a fellow employee, Gilmore finds another job. He soon falls into a pattern of drinking, using drugs, shoplifting, missing work, and starting fights—fights that he invariably loses. He also begins a stormy romance with Nicole Barrett, a nineteen-year-old mother of two who had been married three times. They eventually move in together, but after a few weeks Nicole breaks off the relationship and goes into hiding, apparently because she is afraid of Gilmore's violent temper. She is soon seeing other men, and Gilmore's behavior becomes increasingly erratic. He is arrested for stealing a car stereo and is seen with a cache of stolen handguns. On the night of July 19, 1976, a few days before a court appearance that could send him back to prison for violating the conditions of his parole, Gilmore robs a service station in Orem, Utah. He takes a small amount of cash from the attendant, Max David Jensen, a twenty-four-year-old law student, husband, and father, and then forces Jensen to lie face down on the bathroom floor. After shooting Jensen twice in the back of the head, Gilmore takes Nicole's mentally disturbed younger sister to a drive-in movie and later to a hotel. The next night he robs a motel and murders the attendant, twenty-five-year-old Bennie Bushnell, as Bushnell's pregnant wife and child relax in the next room. As he walks away from the crime scene, Gilmore tries to dispose of the murder weapon and accidentally shoots himself in the hand. Within hours, he is captured and jailed.

In the ensuing weeks, Gilmore is transformed from obscure small-time hood into an international celebrity. He first gains widespread notoriety when, after being convicted and sentenced to death, he unexpectedly waives his right to appeal and demands that the state of Utah execute him on schedule. Because Utah's post-*Furman* death penalty statutes do not require automatic appeal of death sentences, Gilmore's decision catapults him to the front of the line leading to the death chamber. His apparent remorselessness, his eagerness to die, and the possibility that he might be executed on time create a public platform for Gilmore. He uses this platform to argue his case. When Utah Governor Calvin Rampton imposes a temporary stay of execution, Gilmore publicly denounces him as a "moral coward."

Gilmore's case is soon being covered in the national press. The real media frenzy begins, however, when both he and Nicole make failed suicide attempts on the same day, the day originally set for his execution. Within days, a menacing photograph of Gilmore, manacled and glaring directly into the camera, appears on the cover of *Newsweek*. The words "DEATH WISH" are emblazoned across his chest. The magazine reproduces many photographs of Gilmore and Nicole and several of Gilmore's drawings. The cover story claims that the romance, which had been rekindled after Gilmore's arrest, gave the story a "Bonnie and Clyde patina" (26). Within weeks, Gilmore would sell exclusive rights to his story for one hundred thousand dollars plus a stake in a future book and movie deal.

By the date of his execution, Gilmore had received more than forty thousand personal letters at the Utah State Prison. Within a few months, he was featured, posthumously, in a lengthy interview in the April 1977 edition of *Playboy* magazine. The deal eventually led to Mailer's "true life novel" and to a made-for-television movie bearing the same title.

As Gilmore is presented in the media, in *The Executioner's Song*, and in the memoir *Shot in the Heart* (1994) by Mikal, his youngest brother, he is defiantly unpredictable. His refusal to conform to expectations is especially evident when he is tried for murder; no defense attorney has ever had a more frustrating client. The evidence against Gilmore is overwhelming—even without the inadmissible confession given to one of the investigating officers—and his behavior consistently baffles those around him. Taken to trial, he insists on pleading not guilty but refuses to allow his attorneys to call the only witness who might help his cause. He becomes outraged when the attorneys rest the defense without calling a witness or entering a single piece of evidence. He insists, against their advice, on being allowed to take the stand.

When the judge reluctantly agrees, Gilmore withdraws his request. His behavior perplexes all involved. Prosecutor Noall Wootton was "twice flabbergasted. . . . It was like dealing with a crazy pony who was off on a gallop at every wind" (*The Executioner's Song*, 431). Gilmore is quickly convicted (the jury is out for only eighty minutes), and his erratic behavior continues in the mitigation hearing that decides whether he will be sentenced to death or to life in prison. Gilmore does take the stand during this phase of the trial and even goes so far as to admit that he is guilty. Such an admission might ordinarily increase a jury's sympathy for a convicted defendant, but Gilmore's testimony is so cold-blooded and hostile that it produces the opposite effect. The opening exchange of Gilmore's cross-examination is typical:

> "How did you kill him?" Wootton began.
> "Shot him," said Gilmore.
> "Tell me about it," said Wootton, "tell me what you did."
> "I shot him," said Gilmore with contempt for the question and the man who would ask such a question. [441]

Gilmore's "confession" fails to win sympathy because it is not a confession in the full sense. Before the confession could benefit his cause, he would need not only to admit guilt but also to express remorse and offer some explanation for his actions. Gilmore's unwillingness to provide such a confession demonstrates both a sensitivity to expectations about his behavior and an eagerness to violate those expectations. His most baffling decision, the decision to insist upon his own execution, can thus be seen as the culmination of resistance and defiance.

This pattern of resistance is motivated and shaped in large part by Gilmore's image of himself as a hardened convict. This self-image apparently began to take shape when Gilmore, at fifteen years of age, was incarcerated in Oregon's MacLaren Reform School for Boys. Records from Gilmore's stay, recovered by his brother Mikal, show escape attempts—one that produced him two days of freedom, several stolen cars, and capture after a high-speed dash for the state line. At the reform school Gilmore was also known for getting into fights and for persistently breaking rules. An acquaintance of Gary's, incarcer-

139

ated with him at MacLaren, recalls that Gilmore intentionally got into trouble so that he could remain in the "maximum security" cottage with the toughest inmates. This same man told Mikal Gilmore that Gary had developed a reputation for sadistic brutality and that he was feared by almost every inmate in the facility (157). Gary spent more than eighteen of his last twenty-two years in prison and almost half of that time in solitary confinement for breaking prison rules.

Perhaps no one is more familiar with the intricacies of the penal system than the long-term, state-raised inmate. The stereotypical image of the hardened convict or hardman exhibits relentless, "manly" resistance to the system's power. Hardened convicts explain that prison is designed to break a man, to make him into a "punk." They wear their own steadfast defiance of authority as a badge of honor. A readiness for violence and murder is also an important element of the hardened convict mythos. Jack Henry Abbott, a state-raised, long-term convict who corresponded with Mailer from prison during the writing of *The Executioner's Song*, has written that "in prison the most respected and honored men *among us* are those who have killed other men, particularly other prisoners. It is not merely fear, but respect" (149–50).

Mailer draws on this same folkloric code of prison status when he compares Gilmore to the two killers from Capote's *In Cold Blood*: "in prison terms, [Perry Smith and Dick Hickock] were punks. Gilmore was a real convict. . . . To prisoners the word convict is a term of approbation. It's the equivalent of a good soldier" (Mailer, *Conversations*, 234). For both Mailer and Gilmore, being a "good convict" depends on unflinching defiance of carceral power:

> Yes, a convict has a . . . great sophistication about the power of society to enforce its rules. He also has a great sophistication about those ways in which he can beat society—it's their life-study, after all. I mean, a man who has been in jail more than half his life gets to know an awful lot about how to manipulate society. And in that sense [other convicts] would respect Gilmore, because they would see it as a vast and mighty manipulation. . . . This was going to be an extraordinary manipulation that he could put upon the normal social procedure, which, by that time, of course, had been that when a man was sentenced to death, he put in an appeal, and pretty automatically his death sentence was commuted to life imprisonment. [Mailer, *Conversations*, 235]

Years later, Mikal Gilmore would write of his brother's crusade for death in much the same way, arguing that the public grew to hate Gary, "not for his crimes, but because, in his indomitable arrogance, he seemed to have figured out a method to win, a way to escape" (xi).

This image of sophisticated and effective resistance to carceral power may seem at odds with Gilmore's campaign to die. If that campaign was a ploy, a misdirection intended to delay or halt the execution—as many observers contended it was—it could not have been a more dismal failure. Only fourteen weeks elapsed between Gilmore's sentencing and his death. In trying to account for the astonishing swiftness of judicial process in Gilmore's case, one conclusion is unavoidable. Had Gilmore so chosen, he could have delayed his execution for months or years. He stood a good chance of having his sentence reduced to life in prison. There was even the outside possibility of parole at some future date.

Does the fact that Gilmore hurried his own execution, however, settle the question of resistance? Might the success of Gilmore's campaign be measured by some other standard? It could be argued, for example, that to appeal a death sentence only increases punishment; to suffer for years on death row and then be executed is perhaps a worse punishment than being promptly executed, especially if promptness is more traumatic for one's executioners. Gilmore seems to draw on such reasoning when he first tells his court-appointed defense team of his decision not to appeal: "Gary listened. Then he said, 'I've been here for three weeks, and I don't know that I want to live here for the rest of my life.' He shook his head. 'I came here with the idea that maybe I could work it out, but the lights are on 24 hours a day and the noise is too much for me' " (489). Gilmore's public campaign to die, in addition to seeking speedy resolution, offers a critique of the prison system. His declaration that life in prison is worse than death suggests that serving time in a maximum security penitentiary is an unusually cruel punishment. His life becomes a case study in the failure of our criminal justice system to rehabilitate youthful offenders.

In resisting carceral power, Gilmore seems especially aware of the crucial role played by diagnostic biography. He attempts to hide parts of his life from investigators and psychiatrists and actively misleads the examiners about his "condition." Gilmore struggles most to shield his relationship with Nicole Barrett from official scrutiny. He even forfeits his best chance of avoiding a death sentence by refusing to allow Nicole to testify in his defense: "He would not agree to calling Nicole as a witness. They tried to discuss it. There, in the little visitor's room at County Jail, he did not listen to Snyder and Esplin's argument that they had to be able to make the jury see him as a human being. Who better than his girlfriend could show that he was a man with a good side? But Gilmore would not allow bringing her into the case. 'My life with Nicole,' he seemed to be saying, 'is sacred and sealed' " (376).

Gilmore's sense of privacy seems at least partly to have been motivated by an attempt to avoid diagnosis. The aspect of diagnosis that most disturbs Gilmore is the suggestion that his behavior may be the product of deterministic forces beyond his conscious control. When interviewers suggest that Gilmore shot himself in the hand because of a subconscious desire to be punished, he responds scornfully, "Accidents can happen to psychopaths as easily as anybody else, man" (Gilmore, *Playboy*, 82). When pressed further on the issue, Gilmore grows angry, telling the interviewers to "print what you want after I'm dead. I just ain't gonna go for this psychological bullshit" (178).

Gilmore also rejects any attempt to trace the source of his criminal behavior to childhood abuse, especially abuse at the hands of his mother. In the *Playboy Interview*, which ends with several fragments of conversation that were surreptitiously recorded in the hours preceding the execution, Gilmore's final words express just this sort of denial: "I keep being asked if I love her, if she loves me, if she loved me when I was a baby. Yeah, goddamn it! Yes! I don't want to hear any more fuckin' bullshit that she was mean to me. She never hit me. She loved me and believed in me!" (186).

This statement is exhaustively refuted by Mikal Gilmore. If *Shot in the Heart* has a central thesis, it is that Gary's murders originated in regular and frequent beatings, administered by both his mother and his father, that Gary endured as a child. Mikal portrays his parents as vicious and sadistic. His account of the family's early years is filled with images of bruised and bleeding children, of broken bones and

142

midnight visits to the emergency room. Frank Gilmore, Sr., Gary's father, was an alcoholic who alternately abandoned his family for weeks at a time and took them to live in motels under assumed names while he engaged in elaborate swindles and confidence games. According to Mikal, his mother, Bessie, beat the children with such ferocity that her own mother and sisters often threatened to take them away from her. On one occasion Bessie reportedly was caught trying to suffocate the infant Mikal after she became convinced that something was wrong with him. Juvenile court records and files from reform school provide Mikal with many references to the abuse that he and especially his three older brothers suffered. He also claims that Gary's prison records describe a series of unprovoked assaults on elderly convicts. By insisting, against overwhelming contradictory evidence, that he was never a victim of child abuse and that his mother never even struck him, Gary reclaims the murders as his own.

The fact that Gilmore seems more interested in denying subconscious or psychological motivation than in denying that he is a cold-blooded killer offers a clue about his stakes in the campaign of resistance. Diagnostic criminal biography writes the offender as the product of power, an individual who himself acts less than he is acted upon. It suggests that his actions are determined rather than self-determined. The persona of the hardman provides Gilmore with a countermyth to official versions of his life. This persona allows Gilmore to craft images of himself as wielding power. Gilmore can be seen negotiating these issues in conversation with his cellmate:

> "They keep taking me," said Gilmore, "to be interviewed by psychiatrists. Shit, they come up with the stupidest questions. Why, they ask, did I park my car to the side of the gas station? 'If I parked in front,' I said to them, 'you'd ask me why I didn't park to the side.' " He snorted at that. "I could put on an act, have them saying, 'Yeah, he's crazy,' but I won't."
>
> Gibbs understood. That offended a true man's idea of himself.
>
> "I am telling them that the killings were unreal. That I saw everything through a veil of water. . . . 'It was like I was in a movie,' I say to them, 'and I couldn't stop the movie.' "
>
> "Is that how it came down?" asked Gibbs.
>
> "Shit no," said Gilmore. "I walked in on Benny Bushnell and I said to that fat son of a bitch, 'Your money, son, *and* your life.' " [357]

143

By styling himself a cold-blooded killer, Gilmore writes himself as an active agent who exercises power over those around him and controls the shape of his own life. Against the deterministic models of his life offered by those working both for and against his execution, he asserts autonomy.

We can best interpret Gilmore's apparently senseless actions by regarding his behavior as part of a struggle between biography and autobiography, between determinism and self-determinism. Only through senseless behavior can the hardman prove that he is not conforming to normal standards of reasonable conduct. The dialectic between senselessness, conformity, and Gilmore's erratic behavior becomes clearer in the context of his history of incarceration. From early adolescence onward, Gilmore was subject to an institutional disciplinary power that controlled virtually every detail of his life. Under these conditions of coerced conformity, deviance was the only means by which Gilmore could assert defiance, or his own autonomy. Criminologist Jack Katz argues that the careers of self-styled hardmen like Gilmore exhibit a kind of moral "dizziness":

> The deviant's dizziness is spinning between two poles. On the one side, the pariah cannot rest when he achieves conformity. His deepest fear is not failure in conventional terms, but that success means cowardice. On the other side, he discovers more in deviance than just a refuge. *Being deviant gives him an edge.* . . . As the deviant increasingly appreciates the moral dangers of conforming to conventional rules and reason, he may simultaneously appreciate the transcendent power he might attain through a "senseless" killing. [Katz, 297]

Gilmore's deviant behavior proclaims his defiance of disciplinary forces. His deviant persona may also be useful in other ways and not only because it tends to intimidate. Deviant behavior in Gilmore's life is associated with chaos:

> The way of the hardman is a distinctive response to the chaos faced by virtually all who persist in common crimes. All career criminals, whether their MO is violent or non-violent, recurrently face the threat that victims, their personal associates in various forms of illicit action, or law enforcement agents will suddenly seize control of their lives. . . . Only the hardman's response embraces rather than avoids or succumbs to chaos; the

144

hardman seizes on chaos as a provocation to manifest transcendent powers of control. [Katz, 219–20]

Gilmore's habit of walking out of stores holding unconcealed, unpurchased merchandise illustrates the possibilities inherent in seeming to provoke and instigate chaos. If he gets away with the theft, the sheer audacity of the act tends to impress his companions. If confronted, he finds himself with an opportunity to display his ability to master a potentially chaotic situation.

Gilmore's strategies for maintaining his reputation as a deviant hardman are myriad. He tells horrific stories about the abuses and indignities inflicted on prisoners, both by guards and by other inmates. He steals and then openly displays a collection of handguns. He confronts people while wearing ridiculous ties and hats that fit him poorly, then asks them to judge his appearance. He laughs and talks loudly during movies. He exhibits a tendency to start fights and a willingness to "fight dirty"; he brags about past acts of cruelty. When a fellow inmate asked for a snake tattoo on his neck, Gilmore claims to have given him a penis instead. And he even boasts of committing murders while in prison (although he later admits that these boasts are false):

> Today, Gary began to speak of prison. Now and again he would go on about that. This may have been one of those days. Gary got around to mentioning that he knew Charles Manson.
>
> Name-dropping, Craig decided, blinking his eyes behind his glasses. They were sipping beer, and Gary was a lot braver, Craig observed, when he had a few beers. "In prison, I killed a guy," said Gary. "He was black and big and I stabbed him 57 times. Then I propped him up on his bunk, crossed his legs, put his baseball cap on his head, and stuck a cigarette in his mouth." [127]

The Gilmore that Mailer depicts combines past brutality with present gratuitous and petty cruelty to foster an aura of danger that he then exploits to his advantage.

Gilmore's rewards for styling himself as a hardman take many forms. His relatives in Provo tiptoe around him, often bribing him with money to stay out of trouble and avoiding topics that seem likely to upset him. Gilmore's boss, Spencer McGrath, allows him to miss more work than any of the other employees and even goes out of his way to help Gilmore finance a car. The aura of danger around Gilmore also seems to play an important role in Nicole's attraction to him; when she first sees him, she thinks that he looks "intelligent and yet bad at the same time, like an older guy who could fit into a motorcycle gang" (74).

Gilmore the outlaw draws on familiar elements of folklore and popular culture. Music, film, journalism, and television as well as street and prison culture frequently depict the motorcycle gang member. Gilmore's account of his first release from reform school illustrates how he blends criminal behavior with certain styles of dress and music to identify himself as part of a defiant criminal subculture:

> I was anxious to do everything, like I couldn't burn up energy fast enough. I felt slightly superior to everybody else 'cause I had been in reform school. I had a tough-guy complex, that sort of smart aleck juvenile delinquent attitude. *Juvenile delinquent*—remember that phrase? Sure dates me don't it? Nobody could tell me anything. I had a ducktail haircut, I smoked, drank, shot heroin, smoked weed, took speed, got into fights, chased and caught pretty little broads. The Fifties were a hell of a time to be a juvenile delinquent. I stole and robbed and gambled and went to Fats Domino and Gene Vincent dances at the local halls. [Gilmore, *Playboy*, 74]

Mikal Gilmore corroborates this image, writing of both Gary and brother Gaylen during the fifties: "They dressed in scarred motorcycle jackets and brutal boots. They smoked cigarettes, drank booze and cough syrup, skipped—and quit—school, and spent their evenings hanging out with girls in tight sweaters, or racing souped-up cars along county backroads outside Portland, or taking part in half-assed, small-town gang rumbles. Mostly, they spent their time looking for an entry into a forbidden life—the life they had seen exemplified in the crime lore of gangsters and killers" (129).

Gilmore's identification with the outlaw element of popular culture continues throughout his life. One important model in popular culture for his hardman persona is apparently Ken Kesey's R. P. McMurphy, especially as portrayed by Jack Nicholson in the film version of *One Flew over the Cuckoo's Nest*. Gilmore sees the film at least twice during his release—he even attends a screening moments after the

146

first murder—and he explains to his cousin Brenda that he feels a certain affinity for the film and its protagonist: "He had watched them film it down the road from the penitentiary, watched it right from his cell window. Besides, he told her, he had even been sent over to that very institution a couple of times from the prison. Just like Jack Nicholson in the film. Brought him in the same way, with handcuffs and leg irons" (58). In both book and film, McMurphy is described as the hardened convict and the unrepentant career criminal. McMurphy's physical prowess, his cunning in working the system to his advantage, his loyalty to and leadership of fellow "inmates," and his relentless rejection of authority mark him as a "good convict." It seems likely that Gilmore would identify with McMurphy and would want to be perceived in a similar manner. The film neatly captures Gilmore's dilemma by equating incarceration with lobotomy and by suggesting that McMurphy is better off dead than living in a disciplinary institition. Like McMurphy, Gilmore longs to escape and, unable to do so, finds a kind of freedom in death.

Another important source for Gilmore's hardman persona is Johnny Cash, his favorite singer. Cash, from the time of his emergence as a recording star in the fifties, called himself "the man in black" and associated himself with images of hardened convicts and cold-blooded killers. In one of his earliest hits, "Folsom Prison Blues," he sings of a life of violence and incarceration in a style that mixes lamentation with bravado. Cash carries this hardman persona into his film career, typically portraying western outlaws and gunfighters. His sympathetic stance toward prison inmates, and his willingness to perform for prison audiences, have made him a favorite with the nation's convicts. In 1968 and 1969 he released two live albums recorded in prisons (*Johnny Cash at Folsom Prison* and *Johnny Cash at San Quentin*). On these recordings prisoners can be heard cheering wildly as Cash heckles guards and recounts his own experiences behind bars.

Gilmore often says that he loves Cash's music, and his final gift to his mother is Cash's autobiography, *The Man in Black*, a book about Cash's struggle with drug addiction (866). Both Gary and Mikal recall that, when Gary escaped from prison for a few days of freedom as a fugitive, the brothers spent several hours together listening to Cash's

147

music. Days later, Gary was arrested following a bungled attempt at armed robbery. He was captured within minutes, having been found wandering in a narcotic haze a few blocks from the scene of the crime, and returned to prison with nine years added to his sentence.

Gilmore's identification with Cash is so strong that he asks to speak with the singer by phone before he dies. Cash does call, on the evening before Gilmore is shot, and the two speak for several minutes. Later that night Gilmore records an audiotaped farewell to Nicole in which he jubilantly recounts the conversation: "Johnny Cash knows I'm alive, he knows you're alive, he likes us" (quoted in *The Executioner's Song*, 942).

By associating himself with hardman figures from popular culture like Cash, McMurphy, and the outlaw biker, and by demonstrating a willingness to break the law, Gilmore advertises himself as part of a continuing tradition of defiant and even triumphant criminality. He thus attempts to recast his life, to rewrite a pathetic tale of criminal incompetence and lengthy prison sentences as a more palatable one of romantic individualism and heroic resistance of carceral power. Such a drastic rewriting is possible because within outlaw and prison culture, time spent behind bars can be both a status symbol and an opportunity:

> A heavy stickup man can experience life in prison not as a time out from the joys of street life but as an opportunity to beat the system from within, even while it is pressing down with its most minute controls. In the underground prison economy, in the corruption of the guards, and in the maintenance of the ghetto street culture in rural penitentiaries, there are infinite daily opportunities to ridicule, to corrupt, and to control the most powerful forces of social control. [Katz, 230–31]

Using much of the same information that makes up his prison record, the hardman constructs a countermyth in which success is measured not by one's ability to stay out of jail but rather by one's persistence in demonstrating a transcendent, violent will.

Gilmore's strategy for resisting authority must have seemed familiar to Mailer as it echoed his own writings on crime, art, and the police. Mailer's fascination with hardmen and psychopaths dates at least to the time of "The White Negro." Any discussion of the rela-

148

tionship between *The Executioner's Song* and the diagnostic biography of the capital offender should consider Mailer's continuing dialogue with the literature of psychopathy. Mailer locates the beginnings of that dialogue in his extensive final revision of *The Deer Park* (1955), and his account of that revision[1] describes an epiphany, a sudden and startling recognition that a gulf separates the interests of the publishing industry from his own interests as an artist. He claims that the moment marked a change in his life, and he describes the change in words that recall the self-styling of the hardman:

> I turned within my psyche I can almost believe, for I felt something shift to murder in me. I finally had the simple sense to understand that if I wanted my work to travel further than others, the life of my talent depended on fighting a little more, and looking for help a little less. But I deny the sequence in putting it this way, for it took me years to come to this fine point. All I felt then was that I was an outlaw, a psychic outlaw, and I liked it, I liked it a good night better than trying to be a gentleman, and with a set of emotions accelerating one on the other, I mined down deep into the murderous message of marijuana, the smoke of the assassins, and for the first time in my life I knew what it was to make your kicks. [*Advertisements for Myself*, 217–18]

Mailer proclaims his new outlaw status in "The White Negro," a manifesto celebrating the creative potential of psychopathy. The essay champions a particular kind of psychopath—the hipster—as an "American existentialist." He claims that only the hipster is adequately prepared to live under the ever-present shadow of death through atomic war, concentration camp, or life-negating conformity: "If the fate of twentieth-century man is to live with death from adolescence to premature senescence, why then the only life-giving answer is to accept the terms of death, to live with death as immediate danger, to divorce oneself from society, to exist without roots, to set out on that uncharted journey with the rebellious imperatives of the self. In short, whether the life is criminal or not, the decision is to encourage the psychopath in oneself" (313). In terms that anticipate his later characterization of Gilmore, Mailer finds in psychopathic behavior a blueprint for resisting a dominant discourse that

---

[1] Published in *Advertisements for Myself* (1959).

149

would subjugate him as a "punk" or a "square." Only the psychopath can avoid being "jailed in the prison air of other people's habits" (313).

Prison psychiatrist and popular writer Robert Lindner was perhaps the chief source of Mailer's information on the clinical profile of the psychopath. Lindner and Mailer were friends during the early fifties. Mailer refers extensively to Lindner's work in "The White Negro." Lindner coined the phrase "rebel without a cause" to describe the psychopath, and his 1944 book of the same name documents the "hypnoanalysis" of a young man diagnosed as a psychopath (Lindner claimed that hypnoanalysis, which combined hypnosis with traditional psychoanalysis, could increase both the speed and effectiveness of traditional therapy). Lindner characterizes the psychopath as a "religious disobeyer of prevailing codes and standards," constitutionally "incapable of exertions for the sake of others" (2). Driven by a need for instant gratification and a subconscious desire to be punished, the psychopath occupies the body of an adult but is arrested in an infantile stage of psychological development.

Mailer's "white negro" or hipster appears to be based on Lindner's description of the psychopath, but Mailer rewrites certain important elements of Lindner's model. The most striking difference between the two models is found in their respective interpretations of the psychopath's violent crimes. For Lindner, these crimes are the products of deterministic forces, forces best understood in terms of Freudian psychology:

> It may well be that the protest, aggression and hostility of the psychopath are merely homeostatic adjustments operating to restore a disturbed organismic balance. In other words, it is quite likely that the overt destructiveness of the psychopath is designed to fulfill a need for return to that state of dynamic equilibrium which characterizes the normal condition of man. The titanic internecine strife between analytically determined drives or needs and social or superego prohibitions perhaps engenders an amount of tension beyond the bounds of tolerance, to the point where unless it is relieved the organism is threatened with disintegration and destruction. So, in order to restore a balance and achieve a relative quiescence, the personal or social aggression is released with such force that it expresses itself as an attack, a burglary, a murder. [*Rebel*, 12–13]

150

Lindner's profile explains the logic of psychopathic violence without assuming self-awareness on the part of the psychopath. The dynamics of psychological motivation exist "on a subliminal level of apprehension, unreportable directly but always noticeable" (*Rebel*, 10).

Mailer's inversion of Lindner's model turns on this issue of self-awareness. Mailer depicts the crimes of the psychopath as therapeutic acts. He argues that for members of an elite, highly self-aware breed of psychopath, crimes become an active and self-directed alternative to the passive therapy of the psychoanalyst's couch: "Like the neurotic he is looking to grow up a second time, but the psychopath knows instinctively that to express a forbidden impulse actively is far more beneficial to him than merely to confess the desire in the safety of a doctor's room. . . . The psychopath murders—if he has the courage—out of the necessity to purge his violence, for if he cannot empty his hatred then he cannot love, his being is frozen with implacable self-hatred for his cowardice" ("The White Negro," 320). Mailer's hipster is able to become his own therapist because he is both psychopath and "the negation of the psychopath, for he possesses the narcissistic detachment of the philosopher, that absorption in the recessive nuances of one's own motive which is so alien to the unreasoning drive of the psychopath" (316–17). Psychopathic behavior thus represents escape from life as a way of duping power and, paradoxically, as the only means of demonstrating self-control, self-interest, and self-determination in the face of overwhelming biological, behavioral, cultural, political, and psychological forces.

Mailer's philosophical psychopath commits violent criminal acts not as a conditioned response to stress but as a ritualized initiation into a new and wider realm of personal power. The philosophical psychopath destroys his conformist, law-abiding self, casts off traditional morality, and is recreated as a powerful figure of cold-blooded self-interest:

What characterizes almost every psychopath and part-psychopath is that they are trying to create a new nervous system for themselves. Generally we are obliged to act with a nervous system which carries in the style of its circuits the very contradictions of our parents and our early milieu. Therefore, we are obliged, most of us, to meet the tempo of the present and the future with reflexes and rhythms which come from the past. It is

151

not only the "dead weight of the institutions of the past" but indeed the inefficient and often antiquated nervous circuits of the past which strangle our potentiality for responding to new possibilities which might be exciting for our individual growth. ["The White Negro," 318–19]

Like Gilmore, Mailer's hipster is more concerned with denying subconscious or external motivation than with denying the title of cold-blooded killer. For both, the title can be a sought-after symbol of personal power.

The parallels between Gilmore's manifestation of the hardman persona and Mailer's rewriting of the conventional psychopathic profile may account for Mailer's initial interest in Gilmore's story after he read the interview in *Playboy* magazine. In the interview Gilmore sounds very much like the hipster described by Mailer. Gilmore is introduced as someone who poses "puzzling questions about our society by the indications of his high intelligence, his articulateness and his brutal emotional detachment" (69). He is described as an accomplished artist and an "eternal recidivist." Much in his language and demeanor recalls the midfifties cultural battle between criminality and conformity that forms the background of "The White Negro." Like Mailer, Gilmore confesses to having been fascinated with the era's culture of delinquency: "The guys in [reform school] that I looked up to, they were tough, they were hipsters—this was the Fifties" (74). Barry Farrell's introductory note even suggests that Gilmore, like the hipster, undergoes a positive transformation in the wake of his killings, that he transcends his street-punk pettiness and rises "to the one occasion where every misery of his life acquired a surprising new meaning and every bitter turn began to count" (70). According to Farrell, "Gary Gilmore's real life lasted only 78 days, beginning last November first when he told the judge who had presided at his murder trial that he was ready to see it end" (70).

Whether or not Mailer saw in the *Playboy* interview an image of his hipster come to life, it cannot be denied that *The Executioner's Song* makes Gilmore seem much like the hipster figure. The novel, for example, appears to confirm Farrell's contention that Gilmore changes after the murders. Before the murders, Gilmore's behavior appears desperate and destructive, and his boasts are mostly empty. After the murders he seems to act in a self-controlled, dignified manner to orchestrate what he considers a proper death. The novel signals the self-destructive aspect of the killings by linking two ambiguous statements to the two shots that killed Max Jensen: "This one is for me" and "This one is for Nicole" (224). On the one hand, the statements indicate that Gilmore makes Jensen atone for some unnamed crime; on the other hand, they cast Jensen as a surrogate victim in Gilmore's murder-suicide.

Either way, the novel suggests that Gilmore, like Mailer's murderous hipster, "empties his hatred" and so becomes capable of love. This self-transformation is confirmed by Gilmore's subsequent renewal of his romance with Nicole and also by his growing generosity toward family members, friends, and even strangers. All of the deterministic forces acting on Gilmore's life lead him to be one thing, but through a triumph of will (so Mailer suggests) Gilmore creates a different self. Instead of begging for his life, Gilmore accepts his sentence and challenges the state to carry it out. Instead of disappearing quietly into the prison system, he attracts worldwide attention. Instead of dying a pauper, he gains a measure of wealth and hands it out like a generous celebrity.

The similarities between Mailer's past depictions of hardmen and his depiction of Gilmore call into question much of the critical response to the novel. The critics have tended to emphasize the contrast between the novel and Mailer's earlier writings and to focus on the disappearance of the first-person narrator who dominates Mailer's previous works of journalism and nonfiction. John Garvey's assessment of the novel is fairly typical in its emphasis on Mailer's unobtrusive style: "There is a remarkable self-effacement here: Mailer vanishes, to let the book appear" (140). Garvey praises Mailer for reproducing the spoken words of his informants with scrupulous accuracy and also for his compassion and lack of condescension in portraying both killer and victims. Mailer seems to have encouraged this sort of reaction. Just as Capote claims that *In Cold Blood* was written in the spirit of a "strictly aesthetic theory" requiring complete objectivity and accuracy, Mailer claims that the "aesthetic imperative" behind *The Executioner's Song* required him to write as a "photographic

153

realist," presenting facts "with no decoration and no interpretation" (*Conversations*, 269).

If Mailer's depiction of Gilmore recalls his earlier writings on psychopathy, it must also be admitted that *The Executioner's Song* avoids the overt egocentrism and editorializing of those writings. Like *In Cold Blood, The Executioner's Song* proclaims its own objectivity. It is not merely a novel but a "true life novel." It recounts a story that readers can compare with their own recollections of a well-known recent case. The narrative demonstrates its journalistic intent by incorporating long passages from trial transcripts, psychiatric reports, interviews, letters, and news accounts. Even sections not quoted directly can often be linked to a particular witness's voice. We see Gilmore through the eyes of dozens of witnesses and often confront conflicting versions of the same event.

Even the look of the printed page, which isolates brief passages with borders of blank space, suggests a reluctance to connect or interpret the facts. The reader is consequently obliged to sift through contradictory testimony:

> Then the Warden said, "Do you have anything you'd like to say?" and Gary looked up at the ceiling and hesitated, then said, "Let's do it." That was it. The most pronounced amount of courage, Vern decided, he'd ever seen, no quaver, no throatiness, right down the line. Gary had looked at Vern as he spoke.
>
> The way Stanger heard it, it came out like Gary wanted to say something good and dignified and clever, but couldn't think of anything profound. The drugs had left him too dead. Rather than say nothing, he did his best to say it very clear, "Let's do it." [984]

The novel unfolds not as a story told by one person speaking but as a chronologically arranged file containing all evidence and investigative reports connected to Gilmore's case.

The novel also proclaims its own objectivity by calling attention to the machinery of the press and the mass media. Almost half of the one-thousand-plus pages depict the transformation of Gilmore's story into a media event and, by extension, into the novel held by the reader. We see the town's hotels fill with journalists and entrepreneurs. We see people bidding for the right to market Gilmore's story.

We see the market for stories spawn a market for embellishments, exaggerations, and outright lies. By confessing that personal bias, sensationalism, greed, bad memories, and deception may have influenced the construction and marketing of the Gilmore story, the narrator warns the reader to maintain a vigilant skepticism.

The novel's complex handling of point of view, in conjunction with the narrator's apparent silence, complicates any attempt to characterize the relationship between Mailer's writings on the hipster and his depiction of Gilmore. Mailer may have celebrated defiant hardmen in the past, but *The Executioner's Song* appears to balance the hardman's resistant discourse against the dominant discourse of carceral power. The novel allows Gilmore his self-stylings, but it also reprints a "Psychological Assessment" report, signed by Robert J. Howell, Ph.D., that concludes with a diagnosis of "personality disorder of the psychopathic or antisocial type" (379). We hear Gilmore boast of his own toughness, but we also hear testimony contradicting the boasts. Conflicting diagnoses and interpretations are matched one against the other, and no particular version is directly endorsed.

This initial appearance of neutrality, however, does not withstand scrutiny. A careful reading reveals that the narration both shapes Gilmore's character toward a preconceived model and takes sides in the oppositional dialogue between jailer and jailed. Perhaps the best examples of the way the narrative tailors Gilmore to fit the hipster model are suggested by Mailer himself in the novel's afterword. After claiming that the book "does its best to be a factual account" (1051) of Gilmore's activities between his release in April and his execution the following January, Mailer acknowledges that he has several times manipulated the facts. The "old prison rhyme" that opens and closes the novel, for example, turns out to be no old prison rhyme at all but instead a relatively new one that Mailer wrote in the sixties for his film *Maidstone*. This bit of misdirection may seem innocent enough, but it should also be noted that the rhyme, which bears little resemblance to collected prison folk songs, is spoken by a decidedly Mailer-esque psychopath: "Deep in my dungeon / I welcome you here / Deep in my dungeon / I worship your fear / Deep in my dungeon / I dwell / I do not know / if I wish you well." By opening the novel with this "old prison rhyme," Mailer surrounds Gilmore with mystery and makes him seem menacing.

Mailer's other confessed acts of fictionalization seem to have been similarly guided by a desire to ensure that Gilmore meets the hipster's standards for dangerousness, intelligence, and emotional detachment. Mailer explains, for example, that Gilmore's letters were edited much more extensively than any of the other source material. "With Gilmore's letters, however, it seemed fair to show him at a level higher than his average. One wanted to demonstrate the impact of his mind on Nicole, and that might best be achieved by allowing his brain to have its impact on us. Besides, he wrote well at times. His good letters are virtually intact" (1052). Mailer's dissatisfaction with the quality of Gilmore's letters is at odds with his claims about factual accuracy and "letting the facts speak for themselves." It also suggests that he measures Gilmore against some preset standard.

One likely source for such a standard is Jack Henry Abbott. Two years after the publication of *The Executioner's Song*, Mailer wrote the introduction to Abbott's *In the Belly of the Beast: Letters from Prison* (1981), in which Mailer compares the two inmates: "Gilmore had his literary talents, and they were far from nonexistent. Still, he could not supply me with what Abbott offered" (xi). What Abbott offers is an articulate and highly detailed ethnography of prison culture, told from the point of view of the long-term, state-raised convict. Mailer discusses Abbott's influence on the composition of *The Executioner's Song* at length when introducing Abbott's book, but he fails to mention Abbott in the confessional afterword to *The Executioner's Song*. Given the similarities between the two convicts, however, it seems likely that Mailer's enthusiasm for Abbott's letters contributes to his disappointment in Gilmore's. Mailer also admits to taking a "few liberties" in editing, arranging, and altering some of his newspaper sources, although he assures the reader that his intentions are straightforward: "It was not done to make the newspaper copy more arresting or absurd: rather the procedure was to avoid repetition or eliminate confusing references" (1052). These modest statements fail to explain adequately Mailer's decision to reprint, back to back, two brief articles from the November 1, 1976, issue of the *Deseret News*. One details Gilmore's decision not to appeal his sentence. The other reports on failed attempts to contact Harry Houdini's spirit on the fiftieth anniversary of his death (492–93). The juxtaposition is arresting because Gilmore is, according to family legend, the grandson of Houdini by a longtime mistress (323–24) and also other sections of the novel mention Houdini. When Schiller approaches Gilmore for the last time, as Gilmore sits strapped to the death chair, it "was as if he was saying good-bye to a man who was going to step into a cannon and be fired to the moon, or dropped in an iron chamber to the bottom of the sea, a veritable Houdini." Gilmore's final words to Schiller—"you're going to help me escape"—seem formulated in response to Schiller's thoughts (982). By linking Gilmore rhetorically and genetically to the world's most famous escape artist, the novel enhances Gilmore's stature as someone who cannot be contained by carceral power.

To these confessed instances of fictionalization we may add several other examples of editorializing that seem both out of step with the novel's reputation for scrupulous objectivity and designed to make Gilmore seem more dangerous, evil, and violent. For example, the section of the novel describing Gilmore's delivery to the Utah state prison immediately after he has received the death sentence ends with a passage that interrupts that section's flat, literal tone: "Outside the prison, night had come, and the ridge of the mountain came down to the Interstate like a big dark animal laying out its paw" (451). In addition, the sentence exactly repeats one used in an earlier passage describing the first night of Gilmore's parole, when he is driven past the prison on the way from the airport to Provo (15). The repetition of this figure neatly frames Gilmore's three months of freedom, lending a mysterious, almost supernatural aura to his story and even suggesting that his return to prison is fated. Gilmore's stature is in some way elevated by this framing device; his fate appears to be in tune with shadowy, supernatural forces.

Gilmore's stature is similarly elevated through subtle cues in the narrative that seem designed to influence our interpretation of particular characters. For example, the novel's basic unit, consisting of one or several paragraphs separated by line spaces, often ends with suggestive understatement. The closing lines may highlight some element of a character's personality or may reflect Mailer's attitude toward that character. Through editing and careful arrangement, the narrative shapes the reader's perception of a character without necessarily altering the character's recorded speech. Mark Edmundson, who comments on this shaping, argues that "one section after another about Gilmore ends with a tonal allusion to his death. The effect . . . is to confer on Gilmore a considerable stature" (441). The same process sometimes works in reverse, so as to diminish a character's stature. When a passage recounting a woman's experiments with hair coloring ends with her claim "Being a redhead is being me" (28), the remark's triteness is underscored by its placement on the page.

These confessed and unconfessed acts of narrative editorializing have the cumulative effect of dividing the novel's characters into opposing groups along lines of self-awareness and conformity. This same binary division is evident in Mailer's earlier writings on the hipster:

> The unstated essence of Hip, its psychopathic brilliance, quivers with the knowledge that new kinds of victories increase one's power for new kinds of perception; and defeats, the wrong kinds of defeats, attack the body and imprison one's energy until one is jailed in the prison air of other people's habits, other people's defeats, boredom, quiet desperation, and muted icy self-destroying rage. One is Hip or one is Square (the alternative which each new generation coming into American life is beginning to feel), one is a rebel or one conforms, one is a frontiersman in the Wild West of American night life, or else a Square cell, trapped in the totalitarian tissues of American society, doomed nilly-willy to conform if one is to succeed. ["The White Negro," 313]

The arch-conformists of *The Executioner's Song* are, of course, the strict Mormons. Characters like Max and Colleen Jensen are represented as squares:

> He never raised his voice and neither did she. If, occasionally, she felt like speaking sharply, she wouldn't. They had decided right from the beginning that they would never leave each other without kissing good-bye. Nor would they go to bed with personal problems unsolved. If they were mad at each other, they would stay up to talk it out. They were not going to sleep even one night being mad at each other.

158

Of course, they also had fun. Stuff like shaving-cream fights. Throwing glasses of water at each other. [213]

The contrast between the description of the Jensens and the novel's account of Gilmore's relationship with Nicole could not be more striking. Gilmore and Nicole have not only arguments but also physical battles. During their last meeting before the murders, Nicole forces Gilmore away from her car at gunpoint. For fun, they take drugs, arrange sexual encounters in public places, and lure a thirteen-year-old girl into their bed.

When Mailer speculates on the possible psychological or "intangible" motives for Gilmore's crimes, he recalls the sharp differences between Gilmore and his Mormon victims: "We were talking about this intense rage that he felt, that he had gotten to the point where he couldn't control it. I think he saw—The Mormons after all are tremendously social-minded people. If we are going to talk about society, Mormons epitomize society. They epitomize society with a great emphasis on cleanliness, order, discipline. And to Gilmore, his getting out of jail and finding it very hard to live in the square world, the Mormons would have been his new jailers" (*Conversations*, 237). *The Executioner's Song*, then, is not as neutral or objective a document as it might initially appear. More important, the novel's "failures" to live up to ideal objectivity seem nevertheless to subscribe to an ideological agenda. By diminishing the stature of those who conform, and by elevating the stature of those who rebel, the novel covertly conveys the same message that "The White Negro" proclaims outright. Mailer finds meaning in Gilmore's crimes by retelling his story as a narrative of incarceration, murder, and redemption. In this retelling, the murders become an inmate's attack on and victory over his jailers.

Once we recognize Mailer's alliance with defiant hardmen, we can critically reassess the novel and its relationship to its subject. In the general discourse surrounding the hardened convict, power involves an oppositional dialogue between the jailers and the jailed. The jailers portray the hardmen as irredeemably dangerous, and the hardmen tell stories that illustrate their own heroic resistance to oppressive power. Gilmore styles himself as a hardened convict and a cold-blooded killer, someone well versed in the art of resisting, avoiding,

159

and manipulating carceral power. The novel supports his view of himself. Both Mailer and Gilmore figure power in terms of this oppositional dialogue, and both find in the resistant discourse of the jailed a model for self-empowerment.

Once we have grasped that Mailer takes a side in the dialogue between jailer and jailed, we must adjust our understanding of the novel and its form to accommodate this resistant stance. Mailer's narrative attacks the dominant discourse on several fronts. In addition to critiquing the prison system by suggesting that it breeds and trains criminals, the novel undermines official diagnostic biography in style and in form. Mailer's exhaustive account of Gilmore's life and behavior makes the official reports of examining psychiatrists, which are reprinted in the novel, appear grossly inadequate. The novel's fractured, seemingly evenhanded viewpoint contrasts with the omniscient, clinically detached gaze of diagnostic biography. Rather than endorse the diagnosis of psychopathy outright, as Capote does in *In Cold Blood*, Mailer identifies the source, including competing opinions, and outlines the value of particular diagnostic conclusions for the state's case. Official psychological reports on Gilmore advance incrementally toward diagnosis and closure, with each piece of evidence lending further support to the final diagnosis. Mailer's novel, on the other hand, avoids closure and seems to court ambiguity and open-endedness.

Even the novel's prose style must be reevaluated as resistant discourse. This style, characterized as simple and scrupulously objective, might also be described as an adaptation of the hardman's own style. Gilmore often recounts tales of prison brutality and cruelty with a flatness of tone that other people find disconcerting and even aggressive. His stories usually end with a punch line that seems designed to shock and to violate the listener's expectations. The following passage, in which Gilmore recalls one of his best friends from adolescence, is typical: "He's a real quiet guy. He never shows how he feels about anything. He's got a good sense of humor. He's pretty passive. He'll go two or three months without even speaking to friends sometimes—just hello, goodbye, I'll see ya. But that being LeRoy, I understand. We both always liked doing the same things—you know, nice cars, good clothes, lots of girlfriends. I shot him one time in the stomach, accidentally" (Gilmore, 72). *The Executioner's Song* also uses this sort of cryptic punch line and in a way that, despite the novel's reputation for scrupulous objectivity, elevates Gilmore and confirms him as a hardened convict.

Considered in light of the hardman's characteristic mode of self-representation, the novel's seemingly simple, objective style acquires sinister meaning. When the first murder is being narrated, for example, the prose combines deadpan delivery and strategic silence in a manner that recalls Gilmore's monotone defiance under cross-examination.

> It was a bathroom with green tiles that came to the height of your chest, and tan-painted walls. The floor, six feet by eight feet, was laid in dull grey tiles. A rack for paper towels on the wall had Towl Saver printed on it. The toilet had a split seat. An overhead light was in the wall.
>
> Gilmore brought the Automatic to Jensen's head. "This one is for me," he said, and fired.
>
> "This one is for Nicole," he said, and fired again. The body reacted each time. (224)

Mailer's stylistic rendering of the killings mimics Gilmore's tough-guy demeanor when he brags about his criminal exploits. Both versions—Mailer's and Gilmore's—are flat and emotionless, delivered in short declarative sentences. Both draw no connections between facts and provide no definitive interpretations. In this sense both can be considered to be working against diagnosis. Mailer's absence as the central figure and narrator, then, may best be understood as his adaptation of the hardman's rhetorical self-presentation.

The cult of the hardman is founded on a rhetoric of defiance. Hardmen define and prove themselves through demonstrations of (and stories about) unrepentant lawbreaking and nonconformity. On these points the myth of the psychopath and the countermyth of the hardman are in agreement. The fact that both sides in this exchange view the hardman as opposing and undermining carceral authority, however, is not enough to make it so. Could the hardman's defiance, for example, be shaped and channeled so that it serves the interests of carceral power? If the chief proponents of a particular resistant strategy are people who are constantly incarcerated, how successful is this strategy likely to be?

161

The style of *The Executioner's Song* draws attention to the fact that the battle over Gilmore's execution is a battle to write Gilmore's biography. Gilmore, the lawyers on both sides, and the journalists, writers, and researchers involved all present versions of his life. Each version is designed to meet certain requirements: the defense team portrays Gilmore as not dangerous enough to execute; the prosecution portrays him as a threat to innocent life. Gilmore's own version invests his crimes with karmic significance and affirms him in his role as cold-blooded, hardened convict. The relationship between Gilmore's autobiography and his official biography, however, is not adequately characterized by images of polar opposition. We must also ask ourselves whether hardened convicts and their self-aggrandizing autobiographies are useful to the criminal justice system.

One way of gauging the success of Gilmore's resistant strategy is to compare his use of his life story with the use of it made by the criminal justice system. Before his trial Gilmore is kept in a cell with another longtime convict, a man named Gibbs. When the two inmates meet, they establish their prison credentials by speaking in jailhouse slang and by exchanging stories about their past crimes. Gibbs claims to have been "on his own" since he was fourteen and to have begun his career as a forger at seventeen when "he wrote and cashed $17,000 worth of checks in a month and bought himself a new car" (354). Gilmore counters by claiming to have broken into at least fifty houses by the time he was fourteen.

> First time Gibbs went to prison out here, he was behind a [$2,500,000] forgery. He took, Gibbs said, 21 counts. Next time he went back was when he blew up a cop's car in Salt Lake. Captain Haywood's car.
> Gave him fifteen years when he was 22, Gilmore said. Did them at Oregon and Marion. Gibbs nodded. Marion had the credentials. Flattened 11 years consecutively, Gilmore told him. Probably four years altogether in Solitary. Gilmore showed real pedigree. [354]

Both Gilmore and Gibbs use their life stories to place themselves near the top of the inmate hierarchy. In the value system of the long-term convict, recidivism and recalcitrance are status symbols. Gibbs says he respects Gilmore because he has served time in the toughest maximum-security prisons without having his criminal spirit broken and because he has killed in cold blood.

Gilmore and Gibbs construct autobiographies in which they style themselves successful, hardened convicts, the sort of men who live by their own laws, kill when necessary, and blow up police cars for fun. If we can see past the mythic and romantic elements in their stories, however, it becomes clear that such autobiographies are useful to the authorities. We see this utility in the most obvious sense, when Gibbs turns out to be a police informant planted in Gilmore's cell to spy on him. In the folklore of the hardman, there is no inmate more despicable or contemptible than the snitch. Gibbs easily gains Gilmore's confidence and friendship, however, and Gilmore goes so far as to include Gibbs in his will. Gilmore misjudges Gibbs because Gibbs demonstrates an intimate knowledge of prison culture and is able to speak in jailhouse slang. The esoteric knowledge and secret language that prompt Gilmore to trust Gibbs prove to be not very secret after all, and the same signs that hardened convicts use to identify themselves to one another can be read as well by guards, lesser prisoners, and even the lowly snitches.

The decision to style oneself a hardman also serves the system's interests in less straightforward ways. When U.S. Attorney Noall Wootton decides to seek Gilmore's execution, his decision is based on Gilmore's history of defiance: "[Wootton] made up his mind to go for Death after looking at Gilmore's record. It showed violence in prison, a history of escape, and unsuccessful efforts made at rehabilitation. Wootton could only conclude that, one: Gilmore would be looking to escape; two: he would be a hazard to other inmates and guards; and, three: rehabilitation was hopeless. Couple this to a damn cold-blooded set of crimes" (304). Gilmore's defiance of authority entails behavior that paradoxically helps prove him dangerous and deserving of maximal punishment. The anecdotes that enhance his status among the inmate population are the same ones that condemn him.

This uneasy relationship between the myth of the psychopath and the countermyth of the hardman is illustrated by the media's representation of Gilmore during the weeks leading up to his execution. *Newsweek*'s cover story on Gilmore, entitled "Death Wish," is typical. It describes Gilmore as a "born-to-lose desperado of that intractable sort known in psychiatry as a sociopath and in the streets as a mindless, heartless, pitiless hard guy" (27). The article portrays him as a cold-blooded monster but also as a highly intelligent and gifted artist. It also says that during his "time on the inside [he] was almost irrepressibly violent" (27) and repeats several stories of horrific violence behind bars, some exaggerated or even fabricated, that Gilmore often told about himself.

Gilmore's insistence on maintaining his status as a hardened convict also sabotages the ability of his defense team to secure him a sentence other than death. Once convicted of murder, Gilmore stands his best chance of escaping the death penalty by showing remorse and convincing the jury that he is no longer so dangerous that he must be executed. Gilmore chooses to be perceived as a cold-blooded killer rather than a petty stickup man pushed to murder by drugs and stress.[2] He refuses to show contrition for his crimes and even seems to taunt the jury just before it retires to decide his fate (445). Gilmore's subsequent decision to waive his right of appeal, which establishes that he is fearless in the face of death, can likewise be seen as serving the penal interests. This decision leads not only to Gilmore's speedy execution but also, albeit indirectly, to the resumption of capital punishment in the United States after a ten-year hiatus.

The uses to which Gilmore's life story is put demonstrate how the would-be hardman can be recruited to participate in the construction of his own damning biography. The criminal justice system places Gilmore in a position, both in prison and on parole, where the easiest route to personal power is that needed to justify his continued incarceration. Within prison, the hardened convict may perch at the acme of inmate status, but he is also the least likely to be released. Outside prison, the long-term state-raised convict is likely to be cut off from all conventional forms of power and status except one: the power created by his reputation as a violent ex-con. Paroled to a small town in working-class, Mormon Utah, a thirty-five-year-old man lacking

---

[2] Katz argues that the cold-blooded or senseless crime represents a "crisis of understanding" for the public as well as the offender: "More generally, when captured and brought into the institutions of modern justice, cold-blooded, 'senseless' murderers face the challenge that to explain their crimes within conventional terms and accept the assistance of psychiatrists or defense lawyers may require abandoning the position of privileged meaning they had given the act" (288).

any of the conventional trappings of power, Gilmore seeks status through public transgression and by advertising himself as dangerous. He wields nonconformity like a club, using displays of recklessness and a violent temper to manipulate those around him and spinning tales of prison brutality to reinforce his image. His behavior does bring him a kind of status, but it culminates rather quickly in a return to prison.

Gilmore defies authority in ways that facilitate his utter subjection to this power. It is therefore difficult to establish an oppositional model of the relationship between carceral power and the self-styled hardman. Gilmore's autobiography and his official biography may be adversarial in terms of rhetoric, but in terms of power and function they are better characterized as collaborative. Both Gilmore and the state set out to prove that cold-blooded murder is a fundamental element of his personality, and they succeed despite the fact that Gilmore reaches the age of thirty-five without killing anyone. The two parties also share an interest in establishing that Gilmore is both legally sane and extremely dangerous. The collaborative model illustrates that psychopathy need not be regarded as a medical condition or even as a diagnosis forced upon a resistant subject. Guided by myths like the myth of the hardman, subjects may cooperate in their own classification.

The myth of the hardman thus collaborates with the criminal justice system by finding rewards in the kind of behavior that, from the point of view of the authorities, merits increased security, harsher punishment, and longer sentences. Gilmore receives some limited practical rewards by playing the role of cold-blooded killer and hardened convict. His ability to intimidate people can be used to advantage, and his willingness to rob and steal often provides him with money and salable merchandise. When he actually becomes a convicted killer, his refusal to discontinue the role, to repent and ask for mercy, brings him the far more significant practical rewards of wealth and fame. Such rewards, however, are atypical. Surely Gilmore could not have anticipated them.

More typically, the rewards for styling oneself a hardman are transitory and intangible. Like the socially disenfranchised who find in ecstatic religion an imaginary realm within which they too may wield

165

power, Gilmore creates a mythic world in which he plays an active and weighty role. After a lifetime of mostly empty boasting, he attempts to make the myth real and to become something other than a small-time hood. He remakes himself to fit what Jack Henry Abbott describes as the state-raised convict's masculine ideal: "Dangerous killers who act alone and without emotion, who act with calculation and principles, to avenge themselves, establish and defend their principles with acts of murder" (15). The largely intangible rewards of playing the hardman are, according to the convict's ethical code, adequate compensation for the much more tangible costs of playing that role.

The myth of the hardman also serves institutional authority by providing a sort of script for would-be hardmen. Gilmore exhibits his knowledge of this script by styling himself a cold-blooded killer long before he actually kills anyone. By claiming to have killed, Gilmore enjoys some of the rewards of hardman status with minimal risk. Gilmore's pattern of reckless lawbreaking while on parole also follows the hardman script; as Katz has argued, the postrelease crime spree fulfills a fantasy common to long-term inmates: " 'state-raised' youths . . . who are confined for much of their adolescence in reform schools, who pass much of their adult lives in prison, and who shape much of their emotions in opposition to the all-encompassing oppression of incarcerative authority . . . generally anticipate, immediately on release, beginning 'escapades' or frenetic involvements with deviance in which they will show scant concern for practical risks" (303). Gilmore corroborates Katz's model in one of his prison interviews: "I came out [of prison] looking for trouble. Thought that's what you're supposed to do" (Gilmore, *Playboy*, 74). In short, playing the role of hardened convict tends to ensure reincarceration.

Gilmore, who died at thirty-six, was incarcerated for twenty-one of his final twenty-four years. The hardman myth impels Gilmore toward deviance in yet another way. Whether he is in prison or outside it, "normal" behavior in a convict is potentially a sign of submission to carceral authority:

> Others may enjoy the peace of playing baseball (or engaging in any other morally inconsequential pursuit) without "just playing baseball." But the

person with an established reputation for deviance understands that his engagement in conventionally routine activities may be taken by any observer, at any moment, as evidence of his performance of the specifically moralized activity, "keeping his nose clean." In a moralized sense, when he is "just playing baseball," he is *never just* playing baseball; he is also, more fundamentally, doing what he is supposed to do, choosing not to be deviant, toeing the line, deferring to normative expectations. [Katz, 296]

Gilmore, who manages to include some form of disruptive, illegal, or antisocial behavior in almost every social encounter, is unlikely to be mistaken for someone "keeping his nose clean." For him, normalcy has been thoroughly stigmatized. He is lured toward deviance as a way of improving on his low social standing and demonstrating that his years in prison have not beaten him into submission.

If the myth of the hardman works in part by offering offenders illusory, intangible rewards for pursuing the hardman's path, then *The Executioner's Song* can be said to perpetuate the myth. The novel suggests that Gilmore purges himself of internal demons through acts of cold-blooded and transcendent violence. After the murders, Gilmore is depicted as having risen in stature. He becomes more capable of love and charity and more able to contain his rage. The novel follows Gilmore's lead in suggesting that his execution represents a kind of victory over penal authority. Gilmore forces the state of Utah to meet his demands, and in the process he attracts attention from the world media and the U.S. Supreme Court. Finally, the novel suggests that Gilmore's actions lead him to fulfillment of his karmic destiny.

An interactionist or collaborative model of carceral power would yield a much different view of Gilmore's story. Such an approach sees Gilmore's crimes not as the product of transcendent willpower, as Mailer does, nor as the product of a fundamentally homicidal nature, as the state does, but rather as an attempt to act out a mythically prescribed role in a particular, nonmythic setting. At the time of the murders, Gilmore's claim to hardman status is becoming increasingly difficult to maintain. In the weeks leading up to the murders, he fails several tests of physical strength. He also starts and then loses at least two fights. He is chronically impotent, and his teenaged girlfriend leaves him, goes into hiding, and begins sexual relationships with other men. At one point she even backs Gilmore down at gunpoint.

In the days immediately preceding the murders, Gilmore's status as a hardman is at its most precarious. He stupidly arranges to purchase a pickup truck that he cannot afford and that will surely be repossessed in a matter of days. He is scheduled to appear in court on charges of theft and violating parole that could return him to prison. In short, Gilmore fails to live up to his own billing. Any power he has enjoyed as a dangerous hardman and ex-convict begins slipping away from him. Cold-blooded murder may or may not fulfill Gilmore's karmic destiny, but it definitely offers him a way to avoid returning to prison as a shoplifter. When Gilmore guns down two innocent men, he finally creates the evidence that proves he is the man he has been claiming to be. The evidence, however, can also be put to other uses.

In romanticizing the hardened convict, *The Executioner's Song* simultaneously supports the myth of the psychopath. The myth is useful not only because it encourages especially defiant inmates to act in ways that ensure and justify their continued incarceration but also because the rhetoric of psychopathy allows for a more generalized policing of the normal. Psychopathy, like the folklore surrounding the hardman, works to link all crime and all nonconformity to the most dangerous of criminals. In this sense, the cult of the hardman and the myth of the psychopath collaborate to shape the response to all crime. The more Gilmore and Mailer advertise their outlaw status, the more they participate in the work of the police.

Perhaps the most important question facing literary critics today is the question of relevance. Too often, the work we do seems strangely disconnected from day to day life and from the concerns of "the real world." This conception of the relationship between literature and society is rooted, at least in part, in what may be called the Great Writers approach to teaching and studying literature. Great Writers have something important to say, and the task facing both scholar and student is the decoding of that message and the appreciation of its form. When we insist on approaching literature in terms of a hierarchy of quality, however, we may fail to appreciate literature as a powerful and active cultural force, a force shaping both the way that individuals perceive the world and the way that societies exercise power.

I have attempted to explore popular narrative as a social force by profiling a largely undocumented and unstudied link between popular narrative and correctional power. At the turn of the century Frank Norris helped naturalize the myth of the born killer, a myth that gave us legalized programs of involuntary sterilization and coincided with a broad expansion of capital punishment. Later, Theodore Dreiser and Richard Wright articulated the same arguments against our system of capital punishment that the Supreme Court would endorse in *Furman v. Georgia*, a decision that temporarily halted executions nationwide. More recently, the befuddled killers of *Native Son* and *An American Tragedy* have given way, at least in popular myth, to hardened, cold-blooded murderers like those described by Norman Mailer and Truman Capote. During the same period, executions have become increasingly frequent, and the nation has embarked on an unprecedented expansion of its correctional system.

I do not suggest that these five novels caused these changes in our nation's practice of capital punishment. I do argue, however, that the novels participate in the creation of myths that play a powerful but generally unacknowledged role in the correctional system and especially in sentencing capital offenders. Bolstered by the rhetoric of scientific objectivity and literary realism, these myths give a comforting certainty to a sentencing process that is at best disturbingly arbitrary, and at worst ripe for the influence of racial and class bias. In doing so, they also provide the criminal monsters that promote the feverish growth of a correctional system that is already of a size unprecedented in the modern world.

BIBLIOGRAPHY

Abbott, Jack Henry. *In the Belly of the Beast: Letters from Prison*. New York: Vintage Books, 1982.

Adams, Randall, William Hoffer, and Marilyn Mona Hoffer. *Adams v. Texas*. New York: St. Martin's Press, 1991.

Anderson, Chris. *Style as Argument: Contemporary American Nonfiction*. Carbondale: Southern Illinois University Press, 1987.

Arlett, Robert M. "The Veiled Fist of a Master Executioner." *Criticism* 22.2 (Spring 1987): 215–32.

Barthes, Roland. "Myth Today." *A Barthes Reader*. Edited by Susan Sontag. Pp. 33–149. New York: Hill and Wang, 1982.

Bedau, Hugo Adam, ed. *The Death Penalty in America*. 3d ed. New York: Oxford University Press, 1982.

Benton, Mike. *Crime Comics: The Illustrated History*. Dallas, Tex.: Taylor Publishing, 1993.

Boyle, Thomas. *Black Swine in the Sewers of Hampstead*. New York: Penguin Books, 1989.

Braggiotti, Mary. "Misery Begets Genius." In *Conversations with Richard Wright*, edited by Keneth Kinnamon and Michel Fabre, pp. 57–59. Jackson: University Press of Mississippi, 1993.

Breuer, Stefan. "Foucault and Beyond: Towards a Theory of the Disciplinary Society." *International Social Science Journal* 120 (May 1989): 235–47.

Byrnes, Thomas. *Professional Criminals of America*. 1886. Facs. ed. New York: Chelsea House, 1969.

Capote, Truman. *Conversations with Truman Capote*. Edited by M. Thomas Inge. Jackson: University Press of Mississippi, 1987.

———. *In Cold Blood: A True Account of a Multiple Murder and Its Consequences*. New York: Random House, 1966.

Bibliography

Cash, Johnny. *The Man in Black*. Grand Rapids, Mich.: Zondervan Publishing, 1975.

Cayton, Horace R. Review of *Twelve Million Black Voices*. In *Richard Wright: Critical Perspectives Past and Present*, edited by Henry Louis Gates, Jr., and K. A. Appiah, pp. 26–27. Amistad Literary Series. New York: Amistad Press, 1993.

Chessman, Caryl. *Cell 2455 Death Row*. New York: Prentice-Hall, 1954.

Cousins, Mark, and Athar Hussain. *Michel Foucault*. Theoretical Traditions in the Social Sciences, ed. Anthony Giddens. New York: St. Martin's Press, 1984.

Darrow, Clarence. *Attorney for the Damned*. Edited by Arthur Weinberg. New York: Simon and Schuster, 1957.

———. *Crime: Its Cause and Treatment*. New York: Thomas Y. Crowell, 1922.

Dawes, Robyn M. *House of Cards: Psychology and Psychotherapy Built on Myth*. New York: Free Press, 1994.

"Death for the Death Penalty?" *Time*, April 2, 1965, p. 62.

Diagnostic and Statistical Manual of Mental Disorders (DSM-IV). 4th ed. Washington, D.C.: American Psychiatric Association, 1994.

DiLeo, Michael. "Writer with Convictions." *Mother Jones*, January/February 1991, pp. 36–38, 81–82.

Dillingham, William B. *Frank Norris: Instinct and Art*. Lincoln: University of Nebraska Press, 1969.

Dreiser, Theodore. *An American Tragedy*. New York: New American Library, 1981.

———. *Tragic America*. New York: Horace Liveright, 1931.

Edmundson, Mark. "Romantic Self-Creations: Mailer and Gilmore in *The Executioner's Song*." *Contemporary Literature*: 31(4) (Winter 1990): 434–47.

Elias, Robert. *Theodore Dreiser: Apostle of Nature*. New York: Knopf, 1948.

Fisher, Phillip. *Hard Facts: Setting and Form in the American Novel*. New York: Oxford University Press, 1985.

Fishkin, Shelley Fisher. "From Fact to Fiction: *An American Tragedy*." In *Modern Critical Interpretations: Theodore Dreiser's "An American Tragedy,"* edited by Harold Bloom, pp. 103–26. New York: Chelsea House, 1988.

Foner, Eric, and John A. Garraty, eds. *The Reader's Companion to American History*. Boston: Houghton Mifflin, 1991.

Foucault, Michel. "The Dangerous Individual." In *Michel Foucault: Politics, Philosophy, Culture*, edited by Lawrence D. Kritzman. New York: Routledge, 1988.

———. *Discipline and Punish: The Birth of the Prison*. Translated by Alan Sheridan. New York: Vintage Books, 1979.

172

Bibliography

————. *The History of Sexuality: An Introduction.* Translated by Robert Hurley. New York: Vintage Books, 1990.

————. *I, Pierre Riviere, Having Slaughtered My Mother, My Sister, and My Brother . . . : A Case of Parricide in the Nineteenth Century.* New York: Pantheon Books, 1975.

————. *Politics, Philosophy, Culture: Interviews and Other Writings, 1977–1984.* Translated by Alan Sheridan and others. New York: Routledge, 1988.

Freeman, Derek. *Margaret Mead and Samoa: The Making and Unmaking of an Anthropological Myth.* New York: Penguin Books, 1984.

Freud, Sigmund. *The Psychopathology of Everyday Life.* Translated by Abraham Brill. New York: New American Library, 1924.

Friedman, Lawrence M. *Crime and Punishment in American Society.* New York: Basic Books, 1993.

Garland, David. *Punishment and Modern Society: A Study in Social Theory.* Chicago: University of Chicago Press, 1990.

Garvey, John. "The Executioner's Song." In *Modern Critical Views: Norman Mailer,* edited by Harold Bloom, pp. 139–42. New York: Chelsea House, 1986.

Gilmore, Gary. "The Playboy Interview." Interview with Lawrence Schiller and Barry Farrell. *Playboy* 24.4 (April 1977): 69–92, 130, 174–86.

Gilmore, Mikal. *Shot in the Heart.* New York: Doubleday, 1994.

Goodman, James. *Stories of Scottsboro.* New York: Pantheon Books, 1994.

Greider, Katharine. "CrackPot Ideas." *Mother Jones,* July/August 1995, pp. 52–56.

Groves, W. Byron, and Michael J. Lynch. *Radical Criminology.* New York: Harrow and Heston, 1986.

Irwin, John. *The Jail: Managing the Underclass in American Society.* Berkeley: University of California Press, 1985.

Katz, Jack. *Seductions of Crime: Moral and Sensual Attractions in Doing Evil.* New York: Basic Books, 1988.

Kinnamon, Keneth. "How *Native Son* Was Born." In *Richard Wright: Critical Perspectives Past and Present,* edited by Henry Louis Gates, Jr., and K. A. Appiah, pp. 110–31. Amistad Literary Series. New York: Amistad Press, 1993.

Krutch, Joseph Wood. "Crime and Punishment." In *The Merrill Studies in "An American Tragedy,"* edited by Jack Salzman. Pp. 10–12. Columbus, Ohio: Charles B. Merrill, 1971.

Lentricchia, Frank. *Ariel and the Police.* Madison: University of Wisconsin Press, 1988.

Lincoln, Bruce. *Discourse and the Construction of Society: Comparative Studies of Myth, Ritual, and Classification.* New York: Oxford University Press, 1989.

Bibliography

Lindner, Robert, M.D. *Rebel Without a Cause: The Story of a Criminal Psychopath.* New York: Grove Press, 1944.

Lingeman, Richard. *Theodore Dreiser: An American Journey, 1908–1945.* New York: G. P. Putnam's Sons, 1990.

Lombroso, Cesare. *Crime: Its Causes and Remedies.* Translated by Henry P. Horton. Modern Criminal Science Series. Boston: Little, Brown, 1918.

Mailer, Norman. *Advertisements for Myself.* New York: G. P. Putnam's Sons, 1959.

———. *Conversations with Norman Mailer.* Edited by J. Michael Lennon. Jackson: University Press of Mississippi, 1988.

———. *The Executioner's Song.* Boston: Little, Brown, 1979.

———. "The White Negro." In *Advertisements for Myself.* New York: G. P. Putnam's Sons, 1959.

Manso, Peter. *Mailer: His Life and Times.* New York: Penguin Books, 1985.

Martin, John Bartlow. *Break Down the Walls: American Prisons: Past, Present, and Future.* New York: Ballantine Books, 1954.

McWilliams, Peter. *Ain't Nobody's Business If You Do: The Absurdity of Consensual Crime in a Free Society.* Los Angeles: Prelude Press, 1993.

Mead, Margaret. *Coming of Age in Samoa: A Psychological Study of Primitive Youth for Western Civilization.* New York: W. Morrow, 1928.

Miller, D. A. *The Novel and the Police.* Berkeley: University of California Press, 1988.

Moers, Ellen. *Two Dreisers.* New York: Viking, 1969.

Nash, Jay Robert. *Bloodletters and Badmen.* New York: M. Evans, 1973.

"Negro Hailed as New Writer." In *Conversations with Richard Wright,* edited by Keneth Kinnamon and Michel Fabre, pp. 28–30. Jackson: University Press of Mississippi, 1993.

Nichols, L. "Mr. Capote." *New York Times Book Review,* 22 August 1965, p. 39.

Nordau, Max. *Degeneration.* 1895. Reprint. New York: Howard Fertig, 1968.

Norris, Frank. *Complete Works of Frank Norris.* 10 vols. Port Washington, N.Y.: Kennikat, 1967.

———. *McTeague: A Story of San Francisco.* New York: New American Library, 1964.

———. "A Plea for Romantic Fiction." *Complete Works of Frank Norris.* Vol. 7. Port Washington, N.Y.: Kennikat Press, 1967.

O'Connor, Flannery. *Three by Flannery O'Connor.* New York: Signet, 1962.

Oppenheim, Janet. *"Shattered Nerves": Doctors, Patients, and Depression in Victorian England.* New York: Oxford University Press, 1991.

Pizer, Donald. *The Novels of Frank Norris.* Bloomington: Indiana University Press, 1966.

———. *The Novels of Theodore Dreiser: A Critical Study*. Minneapolis: University of Minnesota Press, 1976.

Reed, Kenneth T. *Truman Capote*. Twayne American Author's Series. New York: Twayne, 1981.

Reynolds, David S. *Beneath the American Renaissance: The Subversive Imagination in the Age of Emerson and Melville*. Cambridge, Mass.: Harvard University Press, 1989.

Salzman, Jack, ed. *The Merrill Studies in "An American Tragedy."* Columbus, Ohio: Charles E. Merrill, 1971.

Scheffler, Judith A. "The Prisoner as Creator in *The Executioner's Song*." In *Modern Critical Views: Norman Mailer*, edited by Harold Bloom, pp. 183–91. New York: Chelsea House, 1986.

Schleifer, Ronald. "American Violence: Dreiser, Mailer, and the Nature of Intertextuality." In *Intertextuality and Contemporary American Fiction*, edited by Patrick O'Donnell and Robert Con Davis, pp. 121–43. Baltimore: Johns Hopkins University Press, 1989.

Seaver, Edwin. "Readers and Writers." Transcript of a Radio Broadcast: December 23, 1941. In *Conversations with Richard Wright*, edited by Keneth Kinnamon and Michel Fabre, pp. 43–48. Jackson: University Press of Mississippi, 1993.

Seltzer, Mark. *Henry James and the Art of Power*. Ithaca: Cornell University Press, 1984.

Sherman, Stuart. "Mr. Dreiser and Tragic Realism." In *The Merrill Studies in "An American Tragedy,"* edited by Jack Salzman, pp. 17–24. Columbus, Ohio: Charles E. Merrill, 1971.

Skinner, B. F. *The Behavior of Organisms: An Experimental Analysis*. New York: D. Appleton-Century, 1938.

Solomon, Jolie. "Breaking the Silence." *Newsweek*, May 20, 1996, pp. 2021.

Tambling, Jeremy. "Prison-Bound: Dickens and Foucault." *Essays in Criticism* 36 (January 1986): 11–31.

Tompkins, Phillip K. "In Cold Fact." *Esquire* 65.6 (June 1966): 126–27, 166–71.

Trigg, Sally Day. "Theodore Dreiser and the Criminal Justice System in *An American Tragedy*." *Studies in the Novel* 22.4 (Winter 1990): 429–40.

United States Department of Justice. *Bureau of Justice Statistics Bulletin*. "Prisoners in 1994." NCJ-150042. Washington, D.C., 1996.

Valenstein, Elliot S. *Great and Desperate Cures: The Rise and Decline of Psychosurgery and Other Radical Treatments for Mental Illness*. New York: Basic Books, 1986.

Von Drehle, David. *Among the Lowest of the Dead: The Culture of Death Row*. New York: Times Books, 1995.

Bibliography

Walker, Margaret. *Richard Wright, Daemonic Genius: A Portrait of the Man: A Critical Look at His Work*. New York: Warner Books, 1988.

White, Ronald. "The Trial of Abner Baker, Jr., M.D.: Monomania and Mc-Naughten Rules in Antebellum America." *Bulletin of the American Academy of Psychiatry and Law* 18.3 (1990): 223–34.

Wright, Richard. "A Conversation with Richard Wright, author of *Native Son*." Translated by Keneth Kinnamon. In *Conversations with Richard Wright*, edited by Keneth Kinnamon and Michel Fabre, pp. 31–33. Jackson: University Press of Mississippi, 1993. (Originally published in *Romance* [Mexico City] 1 [June 15, 1940], 2.)

———. *Conversations with Richard Wright*. Edited by Keneth Kinnamon and Michel Fabre, pp. 31–33. Jackson: University Press of Mississippi, 1993.

———. *Early Works / Richard Wright*. New York: Library of America, Viking Press, 1991.

———. "How Bigger Was Born." *Native Son*. Restored ed. Pp. 505–40. New York: Harper Perennial, 1993.

———. *Native Son*. Restored ed. New York: Harper Perennial, 1993.

INDEX

Index

Index